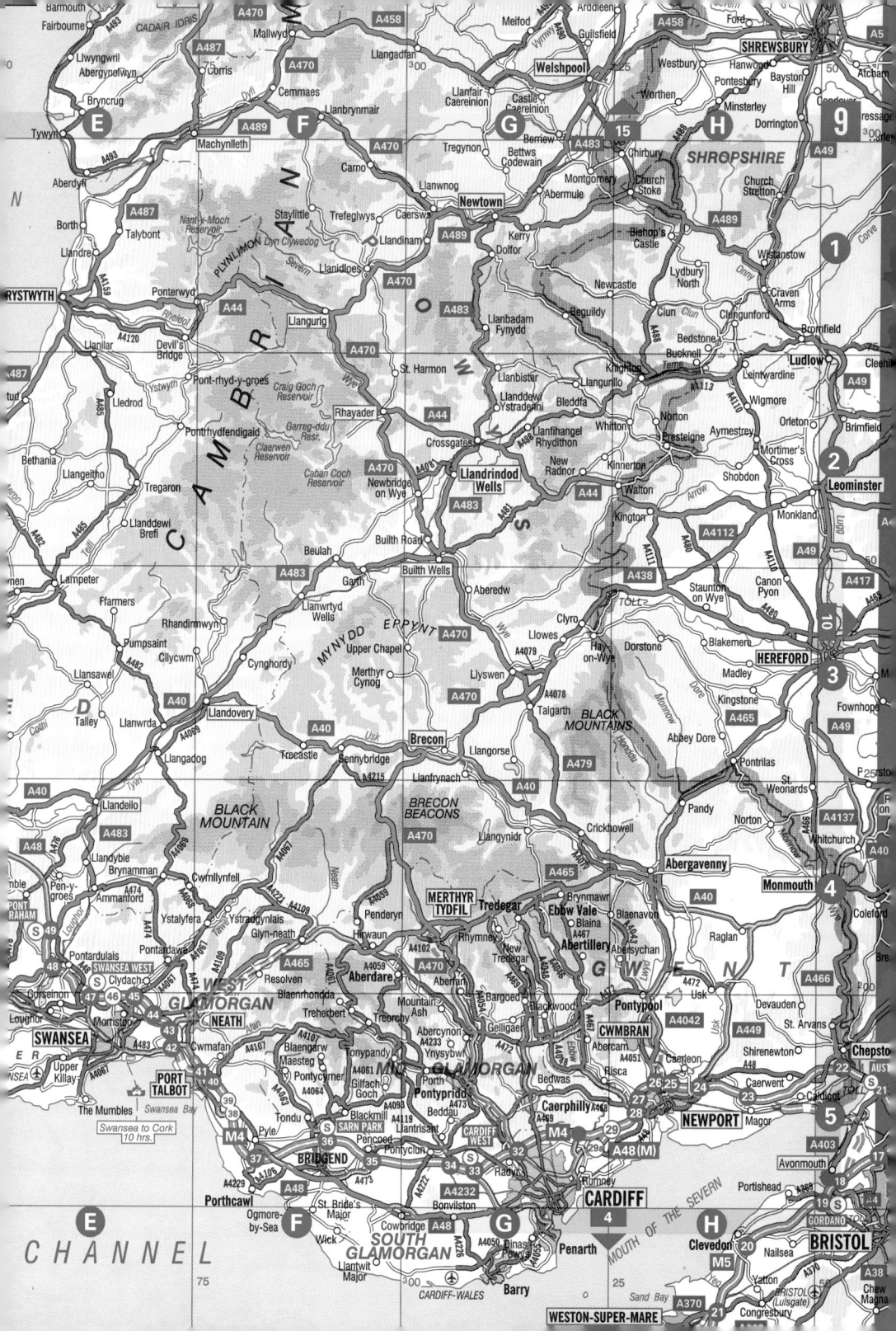

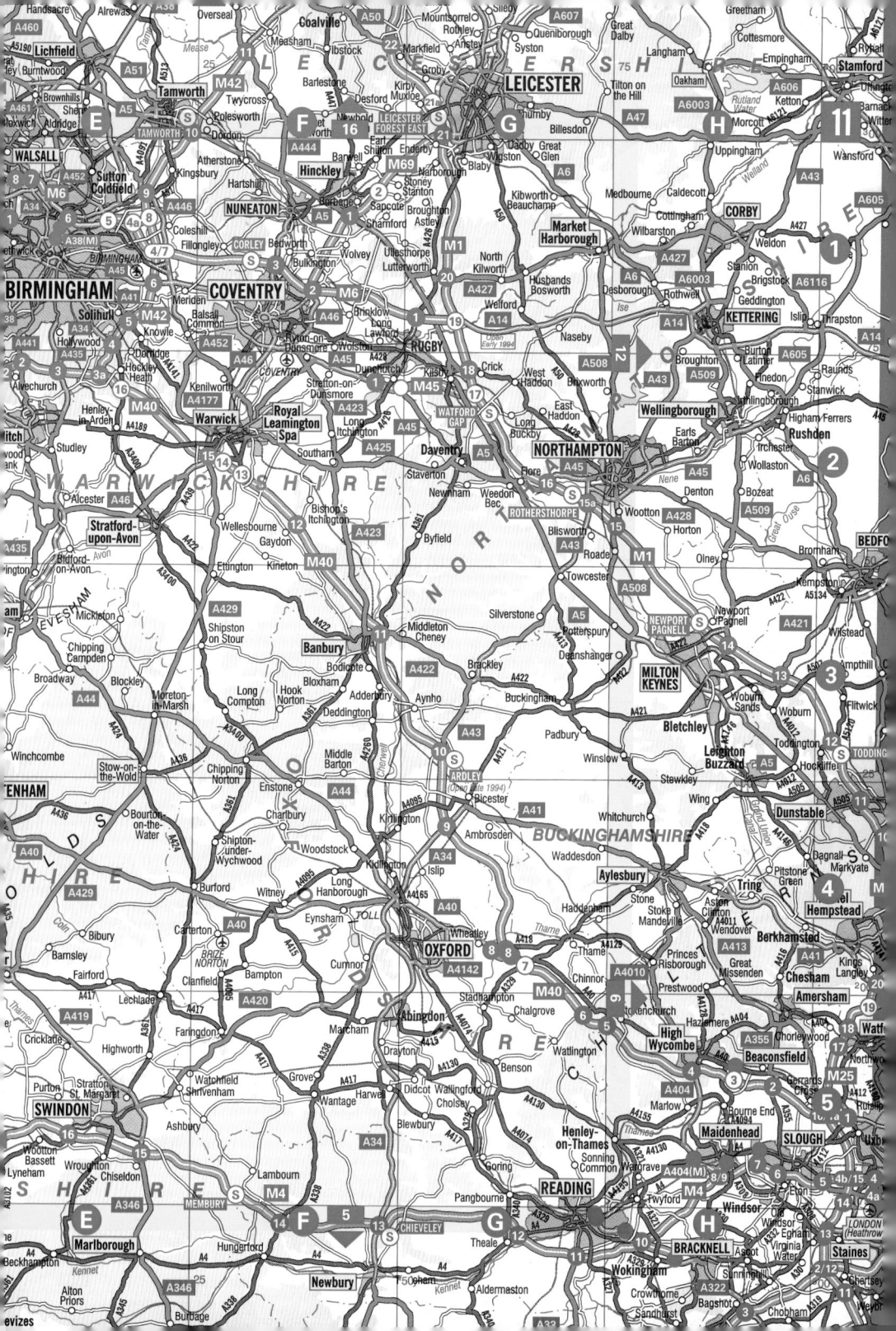

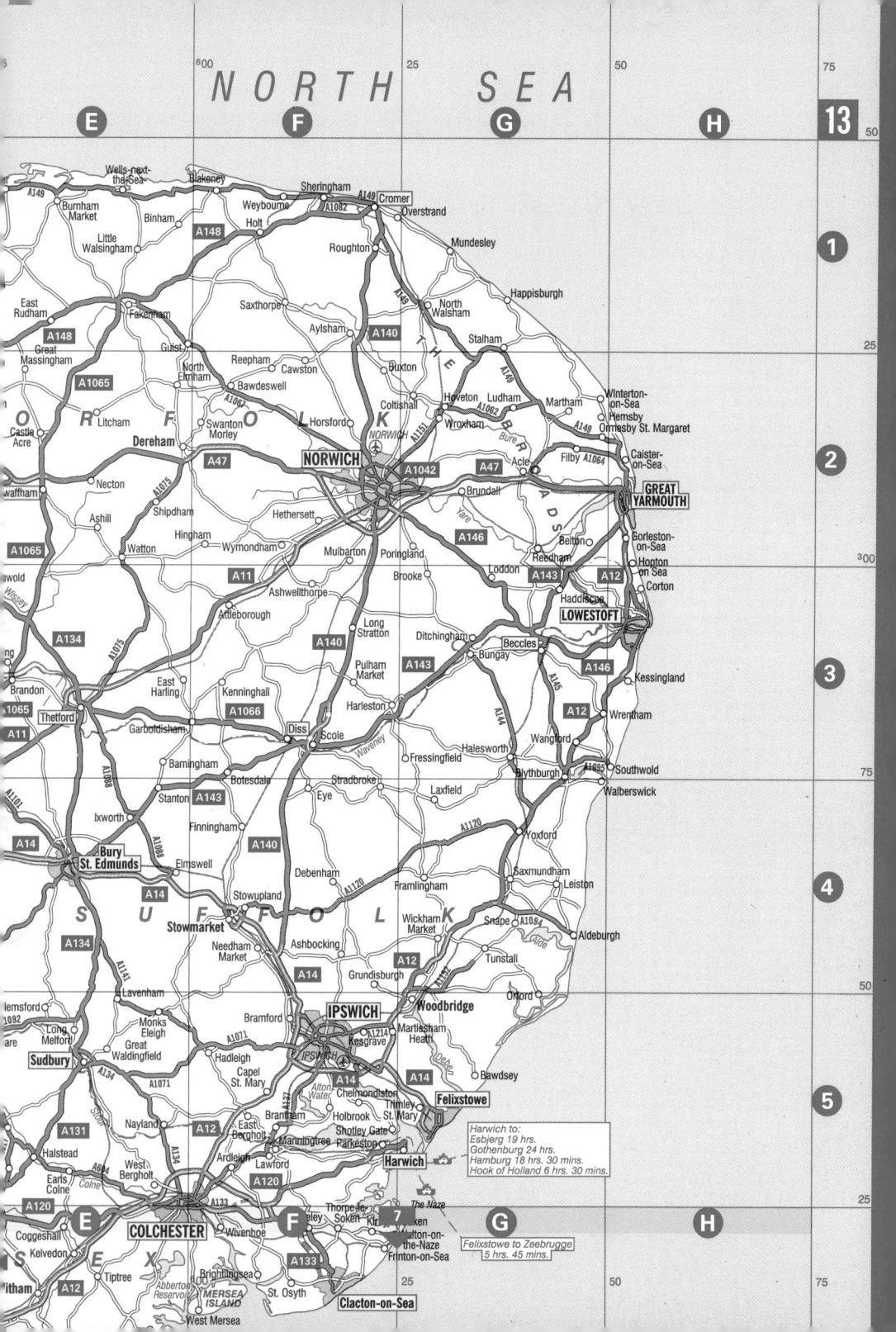

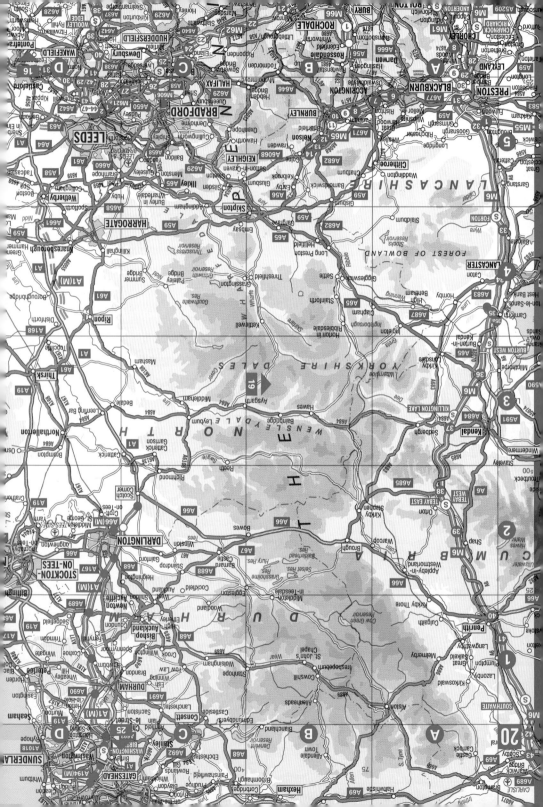

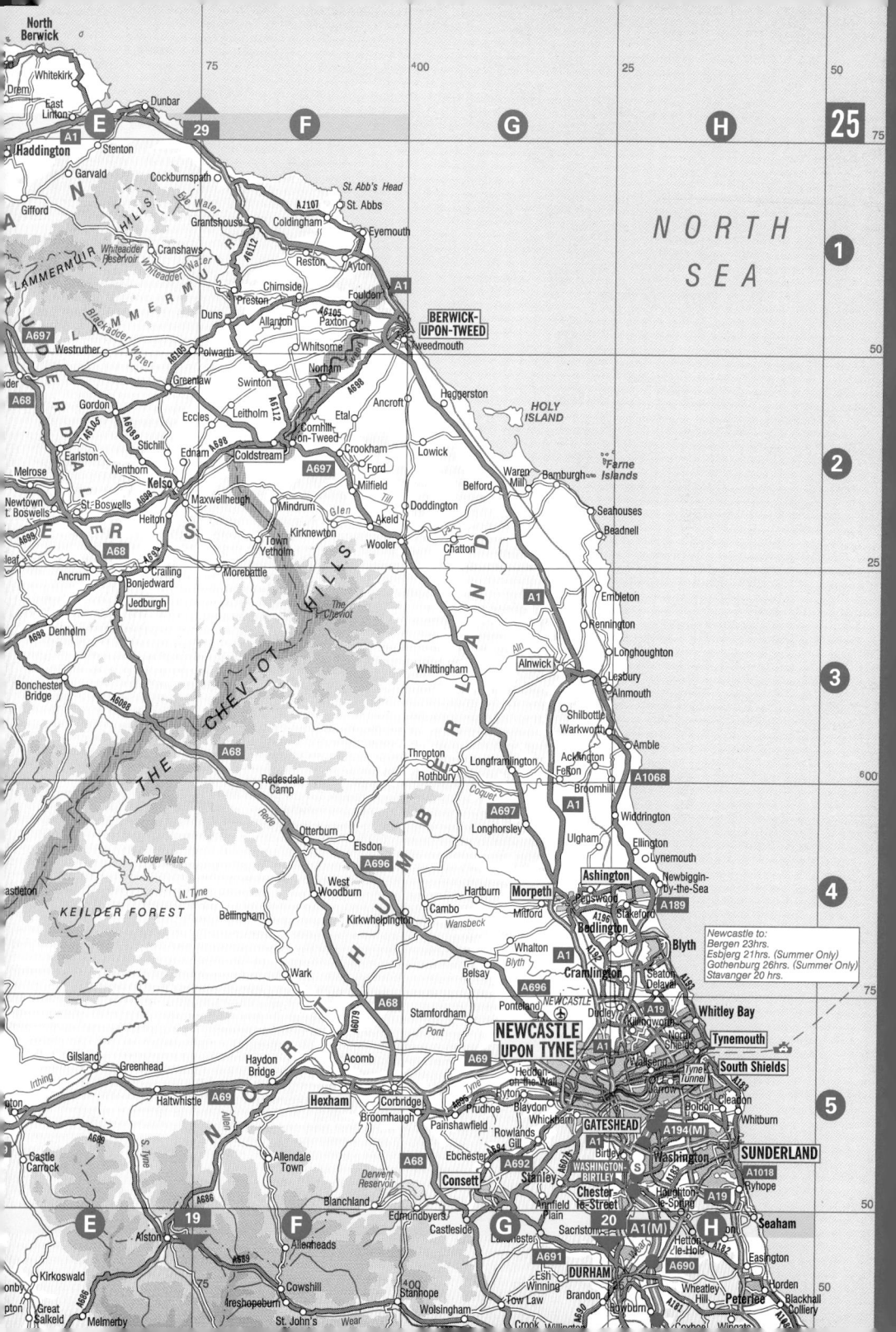

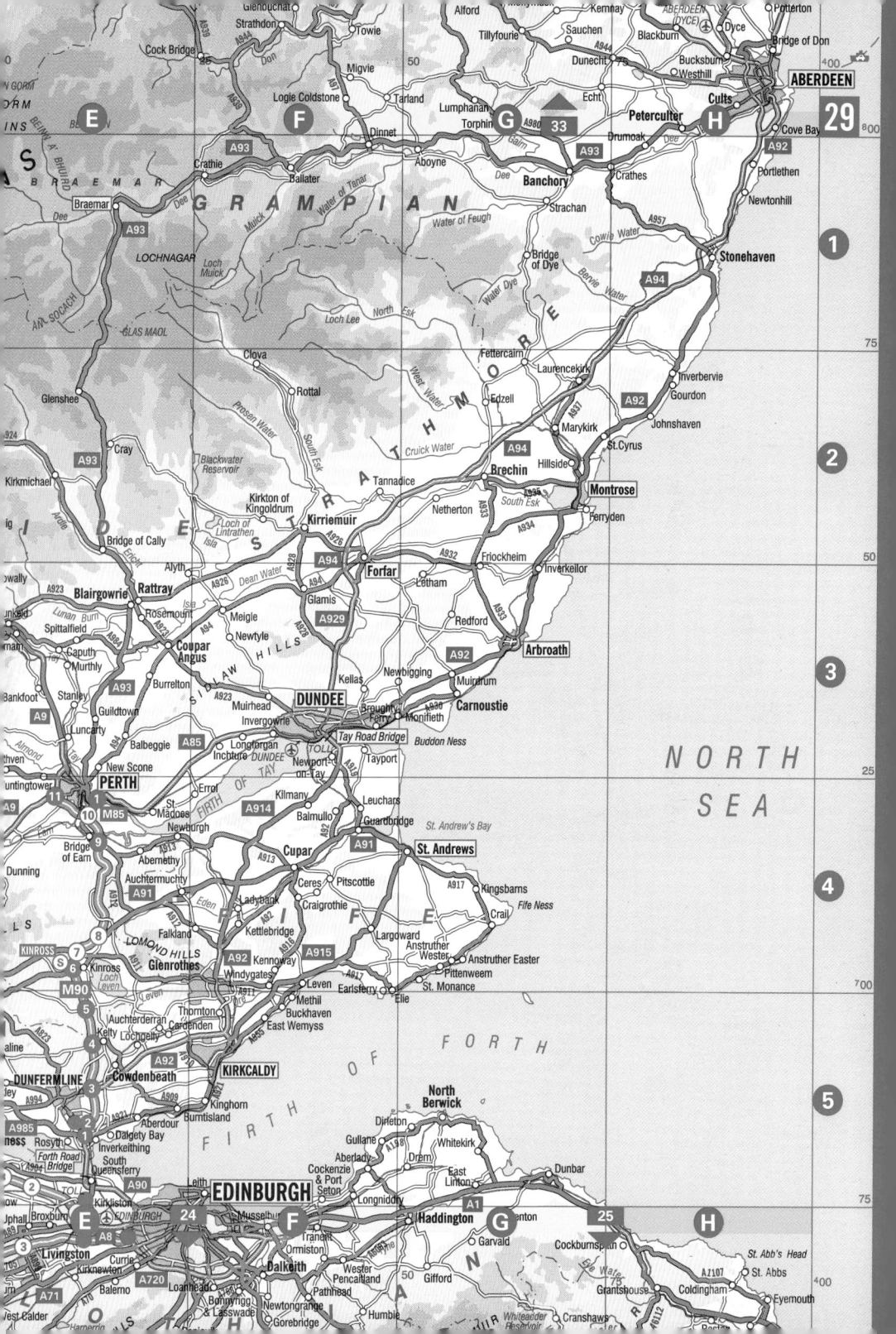

Scarp
Hushinish
Kebock Hea
Eishken
Lemreway
Loch
Shell
Ardvourlie
NORTH HARRIS
Govig
Amhuinnsuidhe
Meavaig
Clisham
Loch
Claidh
Loch
Bhrollum

50   75

900

30

HEBRIDES

Taransay

West Loch Tarbert
Sound of Taransay
Tarbert
Carnach
Loch Seaforth
SOUND OF SHIANT
Shiant Islands
Scalpay
Grosebay
East Loch Tarbert

Toe Head
Loch Langavat
SOUTH HARRIS
Manish

Tarbert to :
Uig 2 hrs.
Lochmaddy 2 hrs.

75

1

Pabbay
Sound of Pabbay
Boreray
Berneray
Borve
Newtonferry

Griminish Point

Northton
Leverburgh
Finsbay
Rodel
Renish Point

Lochmaddy to :
Tarbert 2 hrs.
Uig 2 hrs.

Rubha na h-A

Kilmaluag

Sollas
A865
Loch Fada
Lochportan
Loch Eaval

Tigharry
NORTH UIST
A867
Lochmaddy

Baynead
Loch
nan Eun
Loch Scadavay

Uig to :
Lochmaddy 2 hrs.
Tarbert 2 hrs.

Kilvaxter
Idrigill
TROTTERN
Uig
Garro
A855

Waternish Point

50

2

Sound of Monach

Monach Islands

Baleshare
Samala
Carnish
Locheport

Balivanich
BENBECULA
Grimsay
Baymore
Ronay

BENBECULA

Geary
Earlish
Hallin
Loch
Snizort

Dunvegan Head
Lusta
Greshornish
Claigan
THE STO

Borreraig
Loch Dunvegan
Loch Pooltiel

Milovaig
Lephin
Kensaleyre
Bernisdale

LITTLE

WESTERN

OUTER

3

Creagorry

Ardivachar Point
Loch
Bee
Wiay
Sandwick

West Gerinish

Stilligarry
Lochskipport
Howmore
Loch
Druidibeg
Rubha Rossel

Stoneybridge

THE

MINCH

Ramasaig
Roag
Harlosh

Idrigill Point
Portnalong
Bracadale
Carbost
A863

Talisker
MINGINISH
Dunvegan
Camasta
Bracadale
Carbost
A850

Sligo

25

Beinn M'hor

Loch Eynort

Daliburgh
Lochboisdale
Rubha na Creige
Moire
Loch Boisdale

Lochboisdale to:
Castlebay 1 hr. 30 mins.
Oban 5 hrs.

Eynort
CUILLIN

Loch Eynort
Loch Brittle

HEBRIDES

4

Ludag
Kilbride
Scurrival Point
Eriskay

Sound of Barra

CANNA

Soay Sound
Soay

BARRA

800

Borve
A888
Castlebay
BARRA

Castlebay to:
Lochboisdale 1 hr. 30 mins.
Oban 5hrs.

Sound of Canna

Kinloch
RUM

Vatersay

SOUND OF RHUM

Cleadale

5

Sandray

Sound of Mingulay

Mingulay

SEA OF THE

HEBRIDES

INNER

MUCK

Sound of Eigg

Tobermory to Armade
2 hrs. 15 mins.

75

A   B   C   D

50   75   100   25

Oban to:
Castlebay 5 hrs.
Lochboisdale 5 hrs.

Point of
Ardnamurchan

Achos
A

Coll to:

SHETLAND ISLANDS

UNST

Herma Ness

Haroldswick
Baltasound
UNST
Balta

Cullivoe
Gutcher
Sellafirth · Uyea
Belmont

Oddsta · FETLAR
Noubie · **FETLAR**

Colgrave Sound

YELL

Mid Yell

North Roe

Ollaberry
Ulsta
Burravoe

Esha Ness

Hillswick

Toft

ST. MAGNUS BAY

Firth
Laxobigging

Out Skerries

MUCKLE ROE

Brae

WHALSAY

Laxo
Vidlin
Brough

Hillside
Voe

Symbister
WHALSAY

Papa Stour

Vementry

Sound of Papa

West Burrafirth

Melby

MAINLAND

Tresta
A971

FOULA

Walls

Easter Skeld

Vaila

Veensgarth

The Deeps

Isle of Noss

Ham

Scalloway
Lerwick

BRESSAY

Hamnavoe

West Burra

Starkigarth

South Havra
Mousa

Lerwick to Stromness 8 hrs.

Bigton

Scousburgh

Boddam

SUMBURGH
Toab
Grutness

Sumburgh Head

Sumburgh to Fair Isle
2 hrs. 40 mins.

75 · 400 · 25 · 50 · 75

E · F · G · H

1200

75

50

25

1100

1 · 2 · 3 · 4 · 5

DRIVING NORTH MAP Pages are before this index
DRIVING SOUTH MAP Pages are in reverse order after this index

COUNTIES and REGIONS with the abbreviations used in this index

Billericay. Essx-2D 6
Billesdon. Leic-5D 16
Billingborough. Linc-1B 12
Billinge. Mers-1G 15
Billingham. Clev-2D 20
Billinghay. Linc-3F 17
Billingshurst. W.Su-4B 6
Bilston. W.Md-1D 10
Bilton. Humb-5G 21
Binbrook. Linc-2F 17
Bingham. Nott-4D 16
Binham. Norf-1E 13
Birchington. Kent-3G 7
Birkdale. Mers-1F 15
Birkenhead. Mers-2F 15
Birmingham. W.Md-1E 11
Birnam. Tays-3E 29
Birtley. T&W-5H 25
Bishop Auckland. Dur
  -1C 20
Bishopbriggs. Stra-1G 23
Bishop's Castle. Shrp-1H 9
Bishop's Cleeve. Glos
  -4D 20
  -3D 10
Bishop's Itchington. War
  -2F 11
Bishop's Lydeard. Som
  -3A 4
Bishop's Stortford. Hert
  -1C 6
Bishop's Waltham. Hamp
  -4G 5
Bishopton. Stra-1F 23
Bittadon. Devn-1F 3
Blaby. Leic-1G 11
Blackburn. Grmp-5G 33
  (nr. Aberdeen)
Blackburn. Lanc-5G 19
Blackburn. Loth-1H 23
Blackford. Tays-4D 28
Blackhall Colliery. Dur
  -1D 20
Blackheath. W.Md-1D 10
Blackmill. M.Gl-5F 9
Blackpool. Lanc-5F 19
Blackridge. Loth-1H 23
Blackwaterfoot. Stra-2D 22
Blackwood. Gwnt-5G 9
Blaenau Ffestiniog. Gwyn
  -4C 14
Blaenavon. Gwnt-4G 9
Blaengarw. M.Gl-5F 9
Blaenrhondda. M.Gl-5F 9
Blagdon. Avon-2C 4
Blaina. Gwnt-4G 9
Blair Atholl. Tays-2D 28
Blairgowrie. Tays-3E 29
Blakemere. H&W-3H 9
Blakeney. Norf-1F 13
Blanchland. Nmbd-5F 25
Blandford Forum. Dors
  -4D 4
Blaydon. T&W-5G 25
Bleadon. Avon-2B 4
Bleddfa. Powy-2G 9
Bletchley. Buck-5A 12
Blewbury. Oxfd-5G 11
Blidworth. Nott-3D 16
Blisworth. Nptn-2G 11
Blockley. Glos-3E 11
Bloxham. Oxfd-3F 11
Bloxwich. W.Md-5B 16
Blyth. Nmbd-4H 25
Blyth. Nott-2D 16
Blythburgh. Suff-3G 13
Blythe Bridge. Staf-4H 15
Blyton. Linc-2E 17
Boath. High-3B 32
Boat of Garten. High-5C 32
Boddam. Grmp-4H 33
Boddam. Shet-5G 37
Bodedern. Gwyn-2B 14
Bodelwyddan. Clwd-3E 15
Bodicote. Oxfd-3F 11
Bodmin. Corn-4D 2
Bognor Regis. W.Su-5H 5
Boldon. T&W-5H 25
Bollington. Ches-2H 15
Bolsover. Derb-3C 16
Bolton. G.Mn-1G 15
Bolton-le-Sands. Lanc
  -4F 19

Bomere Heath. Shrp-5F 15
Bonar Bridge. High-2B 32
Bonawe. Stra-3F 27
Boncath. Dyfd-3C 8
Bonchester Bridge. Bord
  -3E 25
Bo'ness. Cent-5E 29
Bonhill. Stra-5B 28
Bonjedward. Bord-3E 25
Bonnington. Kent-4F 7
Bonnyrigg & Lasswade.
  Loth-1D 24
Bontnewydd. Gwyn-3B 14
Bonvilston. S.Gl-2A 4
Bootle. Cumb-3E 19
Bootle. Mers-2F 15
Boreham. Essx-1E 7
Borehamwood. Hert-2B 6
Boreland. D&G-4C 24
Borgue. D&G-1C 18
Borgue. High-5A 36
Boroughbridge. N.Yk
  -4D 20
Borreraig. High-2C 30
Borrowash. Derb-4C 16
Borth. Dyfd-1E 9
Borve. W.Is-4A 30
  (on Barra)
Borve. W.Is-1B 30
  (on Berneray)
Boscastle. Corn-3D 2
Bosherston. Dyfd-5B 8
Boston. Linc-1C 12
Boston Spa. W.Yk-5D 20
Botesdale. Suff-3F 13
Bothel. Cumb-1E 19
Bottesford. Leic-1A 12
Botwnnog. Gwyn-4B 14
Bourne. Linc-2B 12
Bourne End. Buck-2A 6
Bournemouth. Dors-5B 5
Bourton-on-the-Water.
  Glos-4E 11
Bovey Tracey. Devn-3G 3
Bow. Devn-2F 3
Bowburn. Dur-1D 20
Bowes. Dur-2H 19
Bowmore. Stra-1B 22
Bowness-on-Solway.
  Cumb-5C 24
Bowness-on-Windermere.
  Cumb-3F 19
Boyton. Corn-3E 3
Bozeat. Nptn-4A 12
Bracadale. High-3D 30
Bracebridge Heath. Linc
  -3E 17
Brackley. Nptn-3G 11
Bracknell. Berk-3A 6
Braco. Tays-4D 28
Bradford. W.Yk-5C 20
Bradford-on-Avon. Wilt
  -2D 4
Bradwell. Derb-2B 16
Bradwell-on-Sea. Essx
  -1F 7
Bradworthy. Devn-2E 3
Brae. Shet-3G 37
Braemar. Grmp-1E 29
Braemore. High-5A 36
  (nr. Dunbeath)
Braemore. High-1H 31
  (nr. Ullapool)
Brae of Achnahaird. High
  -3E 35
Bragar. W.Is-2B 34
Brailsford. Derb-4B 16
Braintree. Essx-1E 7
Braithwaite. Cumb-2E 19
Bramdean. Hamp-3G 5
Bramford. Suff-5F 13
Bramhall. G.Mn-2H 15
Bramhope. W.Yk-5C 20
Bramley. S.Yk-2C 16
Brampton. Camb-4B 12
Brampton. Cumb-5E 25
Bramshaw. Hamp-4F 5
Brancaster. Norf-1E 13
Branderburgh. Grmp
  -3D 32
Brandesburton. Humb
  -5G 21

Brandon. Dur-1C 20
Brandon. Suff-3E 13
Brandsby. N.Yk-4E 21
Branston. Linc-3F 17
Brantham. Suff-5F 13
Braunton. Devn-1E 3
Brayton. N.Yk-5E 21
Bream. Glos-4C 10
Brean. Som-2B 4
Breasclete. W.Is-2A 34
Brechfa. Dyfd-3E 9
Brechin. Tays-2G 29
Brecon. Powy-3G 9
Bredon. H&W-3D 10
Brenish. W.Is-2A 34
Brentwood. Essx-2D 6
Bretherton. Lanc-1F 15
Brewood. Staf-5H 15
Bride. IOM-2B 18
Bridestowe. Devn-3F 3
Bridge. Kent-3F 7
Bridgend. Grmp-4E 33
  (nr. Dufftown)
Bridgend. M.Gl-5F 9
Bridgend. Stra-1B 22
  (nr. Islay)
Bridge of Allan. Cent-5D 28
Bridge of Cally. Tays
  -2E 29
Bridge of Dee. D&G-5G 23
Bridge of Don. Grmp
  -5G 33
Bridge of Dye. Grmp-1G 29
Bridge of Earn. Tays-4E 29
Bridge of Ericht. Tays
  -2C 28
Bridge of Forss. High
  -4A 36
Bridge of Orchy. Stra
  -3B 28
Bridge of Weir. Stra-1F 23
Bridgnorth. Shrp-1C 10
Bridgwater. Som-3B 4
Bridlington. Humb-4G 21
Bridport. Dors-5B 4
Brierfield. Lanc-5H 19
Brierley Hill. W.Md-1D 10
Brigg. Humb-1F 17
Brighouse. W.Yk-1B 16
Brighstone. IOW-5F 5
Brightlingsea. Essx-1F 7
Brighton. E.Su-5C 6
Brigstock. Nptn-3A 12
Brimfield. H&W-2C 10
Brimington. Derb-3C 16
Brinklow. War-1F 11
Brinkworth. Wilt-5E 11
Brinyan. Orkn-1B 36
Bristol. Avon-2C 4
Brixham. Devn-4G 3
Brixworth. Nptn-2G 11
Broadclyst. Devn-3G 3
Broadford. High-4E 31
Broad Haven. Dyfd-4B 8
Broadmayne. Dors-5C 4
Broad Oak. E.Su-5E 7
Broadstairs. Kent-3G 7
Broadwas. H&W-2D 10
Broadway. H&W-3E 11
Broadway. Dors-5C 4
Broadwindsor. Dors-4B 4
Brochel. High-3E 31
Brockenhurst. Hamp-4F 5
Brockworth. Glos-4D 10
Brodick. Stra-2E 23
Bromfield. Shrp-1H 9
Bromham. Beds-4B 12
Bromley. G.Ln-3C 6
Brompton. N.Yk-3D 20
Brompton Regis. Som
  -1G 3
Bromsgrove. H&W-2D 10
Bromyard. H&W-2C 10
Brooke. Norf-3G 13
Broomhaugh. Nmbd-5G 25
Broomhill. Nmbd-3H 25
Brora. High-3H 35
Broseley. Shrp-5G 15
Brotton. Clev-2E 21
Brough. Cumb-2H 19
Brough. High-4A 36
Brough. Humb-5F 21

Brough. Shet-3H 37
  (on Whalsay)
Broughton. Bord-2C 24
Broughton. Humb-1E 17
Broughton. Lanc-5G 19
Broughton. Nptn-3A 12
Broughton Astley. Leic
  -1G 11
Broughton in Furness.
  Cumb-3E 19
Broughty Ferry. Tays-4F 29
Brownhills. W.Md-5B 16
Broxburn. Loth-1C 24
Bruichladdich. Stra-1B 22
Brundall. Norf-2G 13
Bruton. Som-3C 4
Brymbo. Clwd-3F 15
Brynamman. Dyfd-4E 9
Bryncrug. Gwyn-5C 14
Brynmawr. Gwnt-4G 9
Bubwith. Humb-5E 21
Buchlyvie. Cent-5C 28
Buckden. Camb-4B 12
Buckfastleigh. Devn-4F 3
Buckhaven. Fife-5F 29
Buckie. Grmp-3E 33
Buckingham. Buck-3G 11
Buckland Brewer. Devn
  -1E 3
Bucknell. Shrp-2H 9
Bucksburn. Grmp-5G 33
Bude. Corn-2D 2
Budleigh Salterton. Devn
  -5A 4
Bugle. Corn-4D 2
Builth Road. Powy-2G 9
Builth Wells. Powy-2G 9
Bulkington. War-1F 11
Bulwell. Nott-4D 16
Bunbury. Ches-3G 15
Bunessan. Stra-4C 26
Bungay. Suff-3G 13
Bunnahabhain. Stra-1B 22
Buntingford. Hert-5C 12
Burbage. Leic-1F 11
Burbage. Wilt-2E 5
Burford. Oxfd-4F 11
Burgess Hill. W.Su-5C 6
Burghead. Grmp-3D 32
Burgh le Marsh. Linc
  -3G 17
Burley in Wharfedale. W.Yk
  -5C 20
Burnham Market. Norf
  -1E 13
Burnham-on-Crouch. Essx
  -2E 7
Burnham-on-Sea. Som
  -3B 4
Burnhaven. Grmp-4H 33
Burniston. N.Yk-3G 21
Burnley. Lanc-5H 19
Burntisland. Fife-5E 29
Burntwood. Staf-5B 16
Burravoe. Shet-2H 37
  (on Yell)
Burrelton. Tays-3E 29
Burry Port. Dyfd-4D 8
Burscough. Lanc-1F 15
Burslem. Staf-4H 15
Burstwick. Humb-5G 21
Burton Agnes. Humb
  -4G 21
Burton Bradstock. Dors
  -5B 4
Burton-in-Kendal. Cumb
  -4H 19
Burton Joyce. Nott-4D 16
Burton Latimer. Nptn
  -4A 12
Burton upon Stather.
  Humb-1E 17
Burton upon Trent. Staf
  -5B 16
Burwash. E.Su-4D 6
Burwell. Camb-4D 12
Bury. G.Mn-1H 15
Bury St Edmunds. Suff
  -4E 13
Bushey. Hert-2B 6
Buttermere. Cumb-2E 19
Butterwick. Linc-1C 12
Buxton. Derb-3B 16

Buxton. Norf-2F 13
Byfield. Nptn-2G 11
Bylchau. Clwd-3D 14
Cabrach. Grmp-4E 33
Caergwrle. Clwd-3F 15
Caerleon. Gwnt-5H 9
Caernarfon. Gwyn-3B 14
Caerphilly. M.Gl-5G 9
Caersws. Powy-1G 9
Caerwent. Gwnt-5H 9
Cairnryan. D&G-5E 23
Caister-on-Sea. Norf-2H 13
Caistor. Linc-1F 17
Caldbeck. Cumb-1F 19
Caldecott. Leic-3A 12
Caldercruix. Stra-1H 23
Caldicot. Gwnt-5H 9
Callander. Cent-4C 28
Callanish. W.Is-2A 34
Callington. Corn-4E 3
Calne. Wilt-2D 4
Calver. Derb-3B 16
Calverton. Nott-3D 16
Camastianavaig. High
  -3E 31
Camber. E.Su-5E 7
Camberley. Surr-3A 6
Camblesforth. N.Yk-5E 21
Cambo. Nmbd-4G 25
Camborne. Corn-5B 2
Cambridge. Camb-4C 12
Camden. G.Ln-2C 6
Camelford. Corn-3D 2
Campbeltown. Stra-3C 22
Camrose. Dyfd-4B 8
Camusnagaul. High-1G 31
  (nr. Loch Broom)
Cannich. High-4A 32
Cannington. Som-3B 4
Cannock. Staf-5H 15
Canonbie. D&G-4D 24
Canon Pyon. H&W-3H 9
Canterbury. Kent-3F 7
Canvey Island. Essx-2E 7
Capel. Surr-4B 6
Capel St Mary. Suff-5F 13
Caputh. Tays-3E 29
Carbost. High-3D 30
  (nr. Loch Harport)
Carbost. High-3D 30
  (nr. Portree)
Cardenden. Fife-5E 29
Cardiff. S.Gl-5G 9
Cardigan. Dyfd-3C 8
Cardross. Stra-5B 28
Carlisle. Cumb-5D 24
Carloway. W.Is-2A 34
Carlton. N.Yk-1D 16
Carlton. Nott-4D 16
Carlton in Lindrick. Nott
  -2D 16
Carluke. Stra-1H 23
Carmarthen. Dyfd-4D 8
Carnach. W.Is-1C 30
Carnforth. Lanc-4G 19
Carnish. W.Is-2B 30
Carno. Powy-1F 9
Carnoustie. Tays-3G 29
Carnwath. Stra-2H 23
Carradale. Stra-3D 22
Carrbridge. High-5C 32
Carrick Castle. Stra-5F 27
Carronbridge. D&G-4H 23
Carskiey. Stra-3C 22
Carsluith. D&G-5F 23
Carsphairn. D&G-4G 23
Carstairs. Stra-2H 23
Carterton. Oxfd-4F 11
Castle Acre. Norf-2F 13
Castlebay. W.Is-5A 30
Castle Caereinion. Powy
  -5E 15
Castle Carrock. Cumb
  -5E 25
Castle Cary. Som-3C 4
Castle Donington. Leic
  -4C 16
Castle Douglas. D&G
  -5H 23
Castleford. W.Yk-5D 20

Castlemartin. Dyfd-5B 8
Castleside. Dur-1C 20
Castleton. Derb-2B 16
Castleton. N.Yk-2E 21
Castletown. High-4A 36
Castletown. IOM-4B 18
Caterham. Surr-3C 6
Caton. Lanc-4G 19
Catrine. Stra-2G 23
Catterall. Lanc-5F 19
Catterick. N.Yk-3C 20
Catterick Garrison. N.Yk
  -3C 20
Caulkerbush. D&G-5H 23
Cawdor. High-3C 32
Cawood. N.Yk-5E 21
Cawston. Norf-1F 13
Caythorpe. Linc-1A 12
Cayton. N.Yk-3G 21
Cemaes. Gwyn-2B 14
Cemmaes. Powy-5D 14
Ceres. Fife-4F 29
Cerne Abbas. Dors-4C 4
Cerrigydrudion. Clwd
  -4D 14
Chadderton. G.Mn-1H 15
Chagford. Devn-3F 3
Chalgrove. Oxfd-5G 11
Challock. Kent-3F 7
Chapel-en-le-Frith. Derb
  -2B 16
Chapel St Leonards. Linc
  -3H 17
Chapeltown. Grmp-5D 32
Chapeltown. S.Yk-2C 16
Chard. Som-4B 4
Charing. Kent-4E 7
Charlbury. Oxfd-4F 11
Charlestown. Corn-4D 2
Charlestown of Aberlour.
  Grmp-4D 33
Chatburn. Lanc-5H 19
Chatham. Kent-3E 7
Chatteris. Camb-3C 12
Chatton. Nmbd-2G 25
Chawleigh. Devn-2F 3
Cheadle. G.Mn-2H 15
Cheadle. Staf-4H 15
Cheddar. Som-2B 4
Chelmondiston. Suff-5F 13
Chelmsford. Essx-1D 6
Cheltenham. Glos-4D 10
Chepstow. Gwnt-5C 10
Chertsey. Surr-3B 6
Chesham. Buck-1A 6
Cheshunt. Hert-1C 6
Chester. Ches-3F 15
Chesterfield. Derb-3C 16
Chester-le-Street. Dur
  -1D 20
Chew Magna. Avon-2C 4
Chewton Mendip. Som
  -2C 4
Chichester. W.Su-5A 6
Chiddingfold. Surr-4A 6
Chideock. Dors-5B 4
Chilham. Kent-3F 7
Chinnor. Oxfd-4G 11
Chippenham. Wilt-2D 4
Chipping Campden. Glos
  -3E 11
Chipping Norton. Oxfd
  -3F 11
Chipping Ongar. Essx-1D 6
Chipping Sodbury. Avon
  -5C 10
Chirbury. Shrp-1H 9
Chirk. Clwd-4F 15
Chirnside. Bord-1F 25
Chiseldon. Wilt-5E 11
Chitterne. Wilt-3D 4
Chobham. Surr-3A 6
Cholsey. Oxfd-5G 11
Chop Gate. N.Yk-3E 21
Chorley. Lanc-1G 15
Chorleywood. Hert-2B 6
Christchurch. Dors-5E 5
Chudleigh. Devn-3G 3
Chulmleigh. Devn-2F 3
Church Stoke. Powy-1H 9
Church Stretton. Shrp
  -1H 9

Chwilog. Gwyn-4B 14
Cilycwm. Dyfd-3F 9
Cinderford. Glos-4C 10
Cirencester. Glos-4E 11
Clachaig. Stra-5F 27
Clachan. Stra-1D 22
  (nr. Kintyre)
Clachan of Glendaruel. Stra
  -5F 27
Clackmannan. Cent-5D 28
Clacton-on-Sea. Essx-1F 7
Cladich. Stra-4F 27
Claigan. High-2C 30
Clanfield. Oxfd-4F 11
Claonaig. Stra-4D 22
Clapham. N.Yk-4G 19
Clarbeston Road. Dyfd
  -4C 8
Clare. Suff-5E 13
Clashmore. High-2B 32
  (nr. Dornoch)
Clashnessie. High-2E 35
Clatt. Grmp-4F 33
Claverley. Shrp-1D 10
Clawdd-newydd. Clwd
  -3E 15
Clay Cross. Derb-3C 16
Clayton West. W.Yk-1C 16
Cleadale. High-1C 26
Cleadon. T&W-5H 25
Cleat. Orkn-3B 36
Cleator Moor. Cumb-2E 19
Cleckheaton. W.Yk-1B 16
Cleehill. Shrp-1C 10
Cleethorpes. Humb-1G 17
Clenchwarton. Norf-2D 12
Cleobury Mortimer. Shrp
  -1C 10
Clevedon. Avon-2B 4
Cleveleys. Lanc-5F 19
Cliffe. Kent-2D 6
Clifton. Nott-4D 16
Clifton-upon-Teme. H&W
  -2C 10
Clitheroe. Lanc-5G 19
Clola. Grmp-4H 33
Clophill. Beds-5B 12
Closeburn. D&G-4H 23
Clova. Tays-2F 29
Clovelly. Devn-2E 3
Clowne. Derb-2C 16
Clun. Shrp-1H 9
Clungunford. Shrp-1H 9
Clydach. W.Gl-4E 9
Clydebank. Stra-1G 23
Clyro. Powy-3G 9
Coalville. Leic-5C 16
Coatbridge. Stra-1G 23
Coates. Camb-3C 12
Cobham. Surr-3B 6
Cock Bridge. Grmp-5D 32
Cockburnspath. Bord
  -1F 25
Cockenzie & Port Seton.
  Loth-5F 29
Cockermouth. Cumb-1E 19
Cockfield. Dur-2C 20
Codsall. Staf-5H 15
Coedpoeth. Clwd-4F 15
Coggeshall. Essx-1E 7
Colchester. Essx-1E 7
Coldbackie. High-2H 35
Coldingham. Bord-1F 25
Coldstream. Bord-2F 25
Coleford. Glos-4C 10
Coleshill. Warw-1E 11
Colintraive. Stra-5F 27
Coll. W.Is-2B 34
Collieston. Grmp-4H 33
Collin. D&G-4C 24
Collingbourne Kingston.
  Wilt-2E 5
Collingham. W.Yk-5D 20
Colmonell. Stra-4E 23
Colne. Lanc-5H 19
Colsterworth. Linc-2A 12
Coltishall. Norf-2G 13
Colwyn Bay. Clwd-2D 14
Colyton. Devn-4F 3
Combe Martin. Devn-1F 3
Comberton. Camb-4C 12
Compton. W.Su-5A 6

Comrie. Tays-4D 28
Condover. Shrp-5F 15
Congleton. Ches-3H 15
Congresbury. Avon-2B 4
Coningsby. Linc-3F 17
Conisbrough. S.Yk-2C 16
Coniston. Cumb-3F 19
Connah's Quay. Clwd
  -3F 15
Connel. Stra-3E 27
Connel Park. Stra-3G 23
Conon Bridge. High-3B 32
Consett. Dur-1C 20
Contin. High-3A 32
Conwy. Gwyn-2D 14
Cookley. H&W-1D 10
Coombe Bissett. Wilt-3E 5
Copmanthorpe. N.Yk
  -5E 21
Copplestone. Devn-2G 3
Coppull. Lanc-1G 15
Corbridge. Nmbd-5F 25
Corby. Nptn-3A 12
Corby Glen. Linc-1F 17
Corfe. Som-4A 4
Corfe Castle. Dors-5D 4
Cornhill. Grmp-3F 33
Cornhill-on-Tweed. Nmbd
  -2F 25
Corpach. High-1F 27
Corran. High-2F 27
  (nr. Arnisdale)
Corrie. Stra-2E 23
Corris. Gwyn-5C 14
Corry. High-4E 31
Corsham. Wilt-2D 4
Corsock. D&G-4H 23
Corton. Suff-3H 13
Corwen. Clwd-4E 15
Cotgrave. Nott-4D 16
Cottenham. Camb-4C 12
Cottesmore. Leic-2A 12
Cottingham. Humb-5G 21
Cottingham. Nptn-3A 12
Coulport. Stra-5F 27
Coundon. Dur-1C 20
Coupar Angus. Tays-3E 29
Cove. High-1F 31
Cove Bay. Grmp-5G 33
Coven. Staf-5H 15
Coventry. W.Md-1F 11
Cowbit. Linc-2C 12
Cowbridge. S.Gl-2A 4
Cowdenbeath. Fife-5E 29
Cowes. IOW-5F 5
Cowfold. W.Su-5B 6
Cowshill. Dur-1H 19
Coxhoe. Dur-1D 20
Coylton. Stra-3F 23
Craigellachie. Grmp-4E 33
Craighouse. Stra-1C 22
Craignure. Stra-3D 26
Craigrothie. Fife-4F 29
Crail. Fife-4G 29
Crailing. Bord-3E 25
Cramlington. Nmbd-4H 25
Cranborne. Dors-4E 5
Cranleigh. Surr-4B 6
Cranshaws. Bord-1E 25
Cranwell. Linc-4F 17
Crathes. Grmp-1G 29
Crathie. Grmp-1F 29
Crathorne. N.Yk-2D 20
Craven Arms. Shrp-1H 9
Crawley. W.Su-4C 6
Cray. Tays-2E 29
Creagorry. W.Is-3B 30
Crediton. Devn-3G 3
Creetown. D&G-5F 23
Creggans. Stra-4F 27
Cressage. Shrp-5G 15
Creswell. Derb-3D 16
Crewe. Ches-3H 15
Crewkerne. Som-4B 4
Crianlarich. Cent-4B 28
Criccieth. Gwyn-4B 14
Crich. Derb-3C 16
Crick. Nptn-2G 11
Crickhowell. Powy-4G 9
Cricklade. Wilt-5E 11
Crieff. Tays-4D 28
Crimond. Grmp-3H 33

Crinan. Stra-5E 27
Crocketford. D&G-5H 23
Croft-on-Tees. N.Yk-2D 20
Croick. High-2A 32
  (nr. Bonar Bridge)
Cromarty. High-3B 32
Cromer. Norf-1F 13
Cromford. Derb-3C 16
Cromore. W.Is-3B 34
Crook. Dur-1C 20
Crookham. Nmbd-2F 25
Crook of Alves. Grmp
  -3D 32
Crosby. IOM-3B 18
Crosby. Mers-2F 15
Crossgates. Powy-2G 9
Crosshill. Stra-3F 23
  (nr. Maybole)
Crosshouse. Stra-2F 23
Crossmichael. D&G-5G 23
Croston. Lanc-1F 15
Crowborough. E.Su-4D 6
Crowland. Linc-2B 12
Crowle. Humb-1E 17
Crowthorne. Berk-3A 6
Croy. High-4C 32
Croyde. Devn-1E 3
Croydon. G.Ln-3C 6
Cruden Bay. Grmp-4H 33
Crulivig. W.Is-2A 34
Crymmych. Dyfd-3C 8
Cuckfield. W.Su-4C 6
Cuddington. Ches-3G 15
Cudworth. S.Yk-1C 16
Cuffley. Hert-1C 6
Culbokie. High-3B 32
Culcheth. Ches-2G 15
Culgaith. Cumb-1G 19
Culkein. High-2E 35
Cullen. Grmp-3F 33
Cullicudden. High-3B 32
Cullingworth. W.Yk-5C 20
Cullivoe. Shet-1H 37
Cullompton. Devn-4A 4
Culmstock. Devn-4A 4
Culnaknock. High-2F 31
Culrain. High-2B 32
Culross. Fife-5D 28
Cults. Grmp-5G 33
  (nr. Aberdeen)
Cumbernauld. Stra-1G 23
Cuminestown. Grmp
  -4G 33
Cummertrees. D&G-5C 24
Cumnock. Stra-3G 23
Cumnor. Oxfd-4F 11
Cupar. Fife-4F 29
Currie. Loth-1C 24
Cwmafan. W.Gl-5F 9
Cwmbran. Gwnt-5H 9
Cwmffrwd. Dyfd-4D 8
Cwmllynfell. W.Gl-4E 9
Cynghordy. Dyfd-3F 9
Cynwyl Elfed. Dyfd-3D 8

Dagenham. G.Ln-2C 6
Dagnall. Buck-1A 6
Dailly. Stra-3F 23
Dalavaig. High-1H 35
Dalbeattie. D&G-5H 23
Dalchalm. High-3H 35
Dale. Dyfd-4B 8
Dalgety Bay. Fife-5E 29
Dalginross. Tays-4D 28
Daliburgh. W.Is-4B 30
Dalkeith. Loth-1D 24
Dallas. Grmp-3D 32
Dalleagles. Stra-3G 23
Dalmally. Stra-3F 27
Dalmellington. Stra-3F 23
Dalnavie. High-3B 32
Dalreavoch. High-3G 35
Dalry. Stra-2F 23
Dalrymple. Stra-3F 23
Dalston. Cumb-5D 24
Dalswinton. D&G-4H 23
Dalton. D&G-5C 24
Dalton-in-Furness. Cumb
  -4E 19
Dalwhinnie. High-1C 28
Danbury. Essx-1E 7

Danby. N.Yk-2E 21
Darfield. S.Yk-1C 16
Darley Dale. Derb-3C 16
Darlington. Dur-2D 20
Dartford. Kent-3D 6
Dartmeet. Devn-4F 3
Dartmouth. Devn-4G 3
Darvel. Stra-2G 23
Darwen. Lanc-1G 15
Daventry. Nptn-2G 11
Davington. D&G-3C 24
Daviot. High-4B 32
Dawley. Shrp-5G 15
Dawlish. Devn-3G 3
Deal. Kent-3G 7
Deanshanger. Nptn-5A 12
Dearham. Cumb-1E 19
Dearne. S.Yk-1C 16
Debenham. Suff-4F 13
Deddington. Oxfd-3F 11
Deepcar. S.Yk-2C 16
Deeping St James. Linc
  -2B 12
Deeping St Nicholas. Linc
  -2B 12
Delabole. Corn-3D 2
Dell. W.Is-1B 34
Delph. G.Mn-1H 15
Denbigh. Clwd-3E 15
Denby Dale. W.Yk-1B 16
Denholm. Bord-3E 25
Denholme. W.Yk-5C 20
Denny. Cent-5D 28
Denshaw. G.Mn-1H 15
Denton. G.Mn-2H 15
Denton. Nptn-4A 12
Derby. Derb-4C 16
Dereham. Norf-2E 13
Dersingham. Norf-1D 12
Dervaig. Stra-2C 26
Desborough. Nptn-3A 12
Desford. Leic-5C 16
Devauden. Gwnt-5H 9
Devil's Bridge. Dyfd-1E 9
Devizes. Wilt-2E 5
Dewsbury. W.Yk-1C 16
Didcot. Oxfd-5G 11
Dinas. Dyfd-3C 8
Dinas Powys. S.Gl-2A 4
Dingwall. High-3B 32
Dinnet. Grmp-1F 29
Dinnington. S.Yk-2D 16
Dinton. Wilt-3E 5
Dippen. Stra-2D 22
Dipple. Stra-3E 23
Dirleton. Loth-5G 29
Dishforth. N.Yk-4D 20
Disley. Ches-2H 15
Diss. Norf-3F 13
Distington. Cumb-2E 19
Ditchingham. Norf-3G 13
Ditchling. E.Su-5C 6
Docking. Norf-1E 13
Doddington. Camb-3C 12
Doddington. Nmbd-2G 25
Dodworth. S.Yk-1C 16
Dolfor. Powy-1G 9
Dolgellau. Gwyn-5C 14
Dollar. Cent-5D 28
Dolton. Devn-2F 3
Dolwyddelan. Gwyn-3C 14
Doncaster. S.Yk-1D 16
Donington. Linc-1B 12
Dorchester. Dors-5C 4
Dordon. War-5F 15
Dores. High-4B 32
Dorking. Surr-4B 6
Dornie. High-3F 31
Dornoch. High-2C 32
Dorridge. W.Md-2E 11
Dorrington. Shrp-5F 15
Dorstone. H&W-3H 9
Douglas. IOM-3B 18
Douglas. Stra-2H 23
Dounby. Orkn-2B 36
Doune. Cent-4C 28
Dounreay. High-1H 35
Dover. Kent-4G 7
Doveridge. Derb-4B 16
Dowally. Tays-3D 29
Downham Market. Norf
  -2D 12

Downton. Wilt-4E 5
Drax. N.Yk-5E 21
Draycott. Som-2B 4
Drayton. Oxfd-5F 11
Drem. Loth-5G 29
Droitwich. H&W-2D 10
Dronfield. Derb-2C 16
Drongan. Stra-3F 23
Drumbeg. High-2E 35
Drumfearn. High-4E 31
Drummore. D&G-1A 18
Drumnadrochit. High
  -4B 32
Drumoak. Grmp-1H 29
Drymen. Cent-5B 28
Duchally. High-3F 35
Dudley. T&W-5H 25
Dudley. W.Md-1D 10
Duffield. Derb-4C 16
Dufftown. Grmp-4E 33
Duffus. Grmp-3D 32
Duirinish. High-3F 31
Dukinfield. G.Mn-2H 15
Dulnain Bridge. High
  -5D 32
Dulverton. Som-1G 3
Dumbarton. Stra-5B 28
Dumfries. D&G-4H 23
Dunan. High-3E 31
Dunbar. Loth-5G 29
Dunbeath. High-5A 36
Dunblane. Cent-4D 28
Dunchurch. War-2F 11
Duncow. D&G-4H 23
Dundee. Tays-3F 29
Dundonald. Stra-2F 23
Dundonnell. High-1G 31
Dundrennan. D&G-1C 18
Dunecht. Grmp-5F 33
Dunfermline. Fife-5E 29
Dunkeld. Tays-3E 29
Dunlop. Stra-2F 23
Dunnet. High-4A 36
Dunning. Tays-4E 29
Dunnington. N.Yk-4E 21
Dunoon. Stra-5F 27
Dunragit. D&G-5E 23
Duns. Bord-1F 25
Dunscore. D&G-4H 23
Dunstable. Beds-1B 6
Dunster. Som-1G 3
Dunure. Stra-3E 23
Dunvegan. High-3D 30
Durham. Dur-1D 20
Durisdeer. D&G-3H 23
Durness. High-1F 35
Durrington. Wilt-3E 5
Dursley. Glos-5D 10
Duthil. High-5C 32
Duxford. Camb-5C 12
Dyce. Grmp-5G 33
Dyffryn. Gwyn-2B 14
Dyke. Grmp-3C 32
Dymchurch. Kent-4F 7
Dymock. Glos-3C 10
Dyserth. Clwd-2E 15

Eaglesham. Stra-1G 23
Ealing. G.Ln-2B 6
Earby. Lanc-5H 19
Earith. Camb-3C 12
Earlish. High-2D 30
Earls Barton. Nptn-4A 12
Earls Colne. Essx-5E 13
Earlsferry. Fife-4F 29
Earl Shilton. Leic-1F 11
Earlston. Bord-2E 25
Easdale. Stra-4D 26
Easington. Dur-1D 20
Easington. Humb-1G 17
Easingwold. N.Yk-4E 21
East Ayton. N.Yk-3F 21
East Barkwith. Linc-2F 17
East Bergholt. Suff-5F 13
East Brent. Som-2B 4
East Bridgford. Nott-4D 16
East Chinnock. Som-4C 4
East Cowes. IOW-5G 5
East Croachy. High-4B 32
Easter Skeld. Shet-4G 37
Eastfield. N.Yk-3G 21

East Grinstead. W.Su-4C 6
East Haddon. Nptn-2G 11
East Harling. Norf-3E 13
East Hoathly. E.Su-5D 6
East Horsley. Surr-3B 6
East Kilbride. Stra-1G 23
East Leake. Nott-4D 16
Eastleigh. Hamp-4F 5
East Linton. Loth-5G 29
East Markham. Nott-3D 16
Eastoft. Humb-1E 17
East Retford. Nott-2D 16
Eastriggs. D&G-5D 24
East Rudham. Norf-1E 13
Eastry. Kent-3G 7
East Wemyss. Fife-5F 29
East Wittering. W.Su-5H 5
Eastwood. Nott-4C 16
Eaton Socon. Camb-4B 12
Ebbw Vale. Gwnt-4G 9
Ebchester. Dur-5G 25
Ecclefechan. D&G-5C 24
Eccles. Bord-2F 25
Eccleshall. Staf-4H 15
Eccleston. Lanc-1G 15
Echt. Grmp-5F 33
Eckington. Derb-2C 16
Edderton. High-2B 32
Edenbridge. Kent-4C 6
Edenfield. Lanc-1H 15
Edgware. G.Ln-2B 6
Edinburgh. Loth-1D 24
Edington. Wilt-2D 4
Edmundbyers. Dur-5G 25
Ednam. Bord-2E 25
Edwinstowe. Nott-3D 16
Edzell. Tays-2G 29
Eggleston. Dur-2H 19
Egham. Surr-3B 6
Eglwyswrw. Dyfd-3C 8
Egremont. Cumb-2E 19
Eishken. W.Is-3B 34
Elgin. Grmp-3D 32
Elgol. High-4E 31
Elham. Kent-4F 7
Elie. Fife-4F 29
Elland. W.Yk-1B 16
Ellesmere. Shrp-4F 15
Ellesmere Port. Ches-2F 15
Ellington. Nmbd-4H 25
Ellon. Grmp-4G 33
Elloughton. Humb-5F 21
Elmswell. Suff-4E 13
Elphin. High-3B 35
Elrig. D&G-1B 18
Elsdon. Nmbd-4F 25
Elstead. Surr-4A 6
Elswick. Lanc-5F 19
Elvanfoot. Stra-3H 23
Elvington. N.Yk-5E 21
Ely. Camb-3D 12
Embleton. Nmbd-3G 25
Embo. High-2C 32
Embsay. N.Yk-4C 20
Emneth. Norf-2D 12
Empingham. Leic-2A 12
Emsworth. Hamp-4G 5
Enderby. Leic-1G 11
Enfield. G.Ln-2C 6
Enstone. Oxfd-4F 11
Enterkinfoot. D&G-3H 23
Eoropie. W.Is-1C 34
Epping. Essx-1C 6
Epsom. Surr-3B 6
Epworth. Humb-1E 17
Erbusaig. High-3F 31
Eriboll. High-1F 35
Erith. G.Ln-2C 6
Errogie. High-5B 32
Errol. Tays-4F 29
Escrick. N.Yk-5E 21
Esher. Surr-3B 6
Esh Winning. Dur-1C 20
Eskdalemuir. D&G-4C 24
Essich. High-4B 32
Eston. Clev-2E 21
Etal. Nmbd-2F 25
Eton. Berk-2A 6
Ettington. War-3F 11
Ettrick. Bord-3D 24
Etwall. Derb-4C 16
Evercreech. Som-3C 4

Evesham. H&W-3E 11
Ewhurst. Surr-4B 6
Exbourne. Devn-2F 3
Exeter. Devn-3G 3
Exford. Som-1G 3
Exmouth. Devn-5A 4
Exning. Suff-4D 12
Eyam. Derb-2B 16
Eye. Camb-2B 12
Eye. Suff-4F 13
Eyemouth. Bord-1F 25
Eynort. High-3D 30
Eynsham. Oxfd-4F 11

Fairbourne. Gwyn-5C 14
Fairford. Glos-4E 11
Fairlie. Stra-1E 23
Fairlight. E.Su-5E 7
Fakenham. Norf-1E 13
Falkirk. Cent-5D 28
Falkland. Fife-4F 29
Falmouth. Corn-5C 2
Fareham. Hamp-4G 5
Faringdon. Oxfd-5F 11
Farnborough. Hamp-3A 6
Farndon. Ches-3F 15
Farnham. Surr-4A 6
Farr. High-1G 35
  (nr. Bettyhill)
Farr. High-4B 32
  (nr. Inverness)
Fauldhouse. Loth-1H 23
Faversham. Kent-3F 7
Fawley. Hamp-4F 5
Fearnan. Tays-3C 28
Featherstone. W.Yk-1C 16
Felixstowe. Suff-5G 13
Feltham. G.Ln-3B 6
Felton. Nmbd-3G 25
Feltwell. Norf-3D 12
Fenstanton. Camb-4C 12
Fenwick. Stra-2F 23
Feolin Ferry. Stra-1B 22
Ferndown. Dors-4E 5
Ferness. High-4D 32
Ferryden. Tays-2G 29
Ferryhill. Dur-1D 20
Ferryside. Dyfd-4D 8
Fetterangus. Grmp-3G 33
Fettercairn. Grmp-2G 29
Ffarmers. Dyfd-3E 9
Ffestiniog. Gwyn-4C 14
Ffostrasol. Dyfd-3D 8
Filby. Norf-2G 13
Filey. N.Yk-3G 21
Fillongley. War-1F 11
Finchingfield. Essx-5D 12
Finchley. G.Ln-2C 6
Findhorn. Grmp-3D 32
Findochty. Grmp-3E 33
Findon. W.Su-5B 6
Finedon. Nptn-4A 12
Finningham. Suff-4F 13
Finningley. S.Yk-2D 16
Finsbay. W.Is-1C 30
Finstown. Orkn-2B 36
Fintry. Cent-5C 28
Fionnphort. Stra-4C 26
Firth. Shet-3G 37
Fishbourne. IOW-5F 5
Fishguard. Dyfd-3B 8
Fishnish. Stra-3D 26
Fitzwilliam. W.Yk-1C 16
Five Penny Borve. W.Is
  -1B 34
Flamborough. Humb
  -4G 21
Fleet. Hamp-3A 6
Fleetwood. Lanc-5F 19
Flimby. Cumb-1F 19
Flint. Clwd-3E 15
Flitwick. Beds-5B 12
Flookburgh. Cumb-3F 19
Flore. Nptn-2G 11
Fochabers. Grmp-3E 33
Folkestone. Kent-4F 7
Folkingham. Linc-1B 12
Fontwell. W.Su-5A 6
Ford. Nmbd-2F 25
Ford. Shrp-5F 15

Ford. Stra-4E 27
Fordham. Camb-4D 12
Fordingbridge. Hamp-4E 5
Forest Row. E.Su-4C 6
Forfar. Tays-3F 29
Formby. Mers-1F 15
Forres. Grmp-3D 32
Forsinard. High-2H 35
Fort Augustus. High-5A 32
Fort George. High-3C 32
Forth. Stra-1H 23
Fortrose. High-3B 32
Fort William. High-2F 27
Foulden. Bord-1F 25
Four Crosses. Powy-5F 15
Foveran. Grmp-5G 33
Fowey. Corn-4D 2
Fownhope. H&W-3C 10
Foxholes. N.Yk-4G 21
Foyers. High-5A 32
Framlingham. Suff-4G 13
Frampton. Dors-5C 4
Fraserburgh. Grmp-3H 33
Freckleton. Lanc-5F 19
Freshwater. IOW-5F 5
Fressingfield. Suff-3A 6
Freswick. High-4B 36
Friday Bridge. Camb-2C 12
Fridaythorpe. Humb-4F 21
Frinton-on-Sea. Essx-1F 7
Friockheim. Tays-3G 29
Friskney. Linc-3G 17
Frizington. Cumb-2E 19
Frodsham. Ches-2G 15
Frome. Som-3D 4
Fulwood. Lanc-5G 19
Furnace. Stra-4F 27
Fyvie. Grmp-4G 33

Gainford. Dur-2C 20
Gainsborough. Linc-2E 17
Gairloch. High-1F 31
Gairlochy. High-1F 27
Galashiels. Bord-2D 24
Galgate. Lanc-4F 19
Galmisdale. High-1C 26
Galston. Stra-2G 23
Gamlingay. Camb-4B 12
Garboldisham. Norf-3F 13
Gardenstown. Grmp-3G 33
Garelochhead. Stra-5F 27
Garenin. W.Is-2A 34
Garforth. W.Yk-5D 20
Gargrave. N.Yk-4H 19
Garlieston. D&G-1B 18
Garmouth. Grmp-3E 33
Garrabost. W.Is-2C 34
Garros. High-2D 30
Garstang. Lanc-5F 19
Garston. Mers-2F 15
Garth. Powy-3F 9
Garvald. Loth-1E 25
Garvard. Stra-5C 26
Garve. High-3A 32
Garynahine. W.Is-2A 34
Gatehouse of Fleet. D&G
  -5G 23
Gateshead. T&W-5H 25
Gaydon. War-2F 11
Gayton. Norf-2D 12
Geary. High-2D 30
Geddington. Nptn-3A 12
Gedney Drove End. Linc
  -1C 12
Gelligaer. M.Gl-5G 9
Gellilydan. Gwyn-4C 14
Gelston. D&G-5H 23
Gerrards Cross. Buck-2A 6
Gifford. Loth-1E 25
Giggleswick. N.Yk-4H 19
Gilberdyke. Humb-5F 21
Gilfach Goch. M.Gl-5F 9
Gilling East. N.Yk-3E 21
Gillingham. Dors-3D 4
Gillingham. Kent-3E 7
Gilmerton. Tays-4D 28
Gilsland. Nmbd-5E 25
Girvan. Stra-4E 23
Gisburn. Lanc-5H 19
Gisleham. N.Yk-4F 21
Glamis. Tays-3F 29

Glasgow. Stra-1G 23
Glastonbury. Som-3C 4
Glemsford. Suff-5E 13
Glenbarr. Stra-2C 22
Glenborrodale. High
  -2D 26
Glencaple. D&G-5H 23
Glencoe. High-2F 27
Glenelg. High-4F 31
Glenfinnan. High-1E 27
Glengarnock. Stra-1F 23
Glenluce. D&G-5E 23
Glenmazeran Lodge. High
  -5B 32
Glenrothes. Fife-4F 29
Glenshee. Tays-2E 29
Glentham. Linc-2F 17
Glinton. Camb-2B 12
Glossop. Derb-2B 16
Gloucester. Glos-4D 10
Glusburn. N.Yk-5C 20
Glyn Ceiriog. Clwd-4E 15
Glyn-neath. W.Gl-4F 9
Gnosall. Staf-5H 15
Goathland. N.Yk-2F 21
Gobowen. Shrp-4F 15
Godalming. Surr-4A 6
Godmanchester. Camb
  -4B 12
Godstone. Surr-3C 6
Golborne. G.Mn-2G 15
Golspie. High-2C 32
Gomshall. Surr-4B 6
Goodwick. Dyfd-3B 8
Goole. Humb-1D 16
Goonhavern. Corn-4C 2
Goosnargh. Lanc-5G 19
Gordon. Bord-2E 25
Gorebridge. Loth-1D 24
Goring. Oxfd-5G 11
Gorleston-on-Sea. Norf
  -2H 13
Gorseinon. W.Gl-5E 9
Gorstan. High-3A 32
Gortantaoid. Stra-1B 22
Gosberton. Linc-1B 12
Gosfield. Essx-5E 13
Gosforth. Cumb-2E 19
Gosport. Hamp-4G 5
Goudhurst. Kent-4D 6
Gourdon. Grmp-2H 29
Gourock. Stra-5F 27
Govig. W.Is-3A 34
Goxhill. Humb-1F 17
Grain. Kent-2E 7
Grampound. Corn-5C 2
Grangemouth. Cent-5D 28
Grange-over-Sands. Cumb
  -3F 19
Grantham. Linc-1A 12
Grantown-on-Spey. High
  -4D 32
Grantshouse. Bord-1F 25
Grasmere. Cumb-2F 19
Grassington. N.Yk-4C 20
Gravesend. Kent-3D 6
Gravir. W.Is-3B 34
Grays. Essx-2D 6
Great Ayton. N.Yk-2E 21
Great Barford. Beds-4B 12
Great Bircham. Norf-1E 13
Great Broughton. Cumb
  -1E 19
Great Broughton. N.Yk
  -2E 21
Great Clifton. Cumb-1E 19
Great Dalby. Leic-5D 16
Great Driffield. Humb
  -4G 21
Great Dunmow. Essx-1D 6
Great Eccleston. Lanc
  -5F 19
Great Glen. Leic-1G 11
Great Gonerby. Linc-1A 12
Great Gransden. Camb
  -4C 12
Great Harwood. Lanc
  -5G 19
Great Malvern. H&W
  -3D 10
Great Massingham. Norf
  -2E 13

Great Missenden. Buck
  -1A 6
Great Ponton. Linc-1A 12
Great Salkeld. Cumb-1G 19
Great Shelford. Camb
  -4C 12
Great Staughton. Camb
  -4B 12
Greatstone-on-Sea. Kent
  -5F 7
Great Torrington. Devn
  -2E 3
Great Wakering. Essx-2E 7
Great Waldingfield. Suff
  -5E 13
Great Witley. H&W-2D 10
Great Wyrley. Staf-5H 15
Great Yarmouth. Norf
  -2H 13
Greene Hammerton. N.Yk
  -4D 20
Greenhead. Nmbd-5E 25
Greenlaw. Bord-2E 25
Greenloaning. Tays-4D 28
Greenock. Stra-1F 23
Greenway. Dyfd-3C 8
Greenwich. G.Ln-2C 6
Greetham. Leic-2A 12
Gresford. Clwd-3F 15
Greshornish. High-2D 30
Gretna. D&G-5D 24
Greystoke. Cumb-1F 19
Grimsargh. Lanc-5G 19
Grimsby. Humb-1G 17
Grimston. Norf-2D 12
Gringley on the Hill. Nott
  -2D 16
Grizebeck. Cumb-3E 19
Grobister. Orkn-2C 36
Groby. Leic-5D 16
Grogport. Stra-2D 22
Grosebay. W.Is-1C 30
Grove. Oxfd-5F 11
Gruinart. Stra-1B 22
Grundisburgh. Suff-4F 13
Grutness. Shet-5G 37
Guardbridge. Fife-4F 29
Guildford. Surr-3B 6
Guildtown. Tays-3E 29
Guilsfield. Powy-5E 15
Guisborough. Clev-2E 21
Guiseley. W.Yk-5C 20
Guist. Norf-1E 13
Gullane. Loth-5F 29
Gunnislake. Corn-4E 3
Gutcher. Shet-2H 37
Gwalchmai. Gwyn-2B 14
Gwbert-on-Sea. Dyfd-3C 8
Gwyddelwern. Clwd-4E 15
Gwytherin. Clwd-3D 14

Haddenham. Buck-4G 11
Haddenham. Camb-3C 12
Haddington. Loth-1E 25
Haddiscoe. Norf-3G 13
Hadfield. Derb-2B 16
Hadleigh. Suff-5F 13
Haggerston. Nmbd-2G 25
Hailsham. E.Su-5D 6
Halesowen. W.Md-1D 10
Halesworth. Suff-3G 13
Halifax. W.Yk-5C 20
Halkirk. High-4A 36
Hallin. High-2D 30
Hallworthy. Corn-3D 2
Halstead. Essx-5E 13
Haltwhistle. Nmbd-5E 25
Halwell. Devn-4G 3
Ham. Shet-4E 37
Hamble. Hamp-4F 5
Hambleton. N.Yk-5E 21
Hamilton. Stra-1G 23
Hamnavoe. Shet-4G 37
  (nr. Scalloway)
Hamstreet. Kent-4F 7
Handforth. Ches-2H 15
Handsacre. Staf-5B 16
Hanley. Staf-4H 15
Hanwood. Shrp-5F 15
Happisburgh. Norf-1G 13

Harlaxton. Linc-1A 12
Harlech. Gwyn-4C 14
Harleston. Norf-3F 13
Harley. Shrp-5G 15
Harlosh. High-3D 30
Harlow. Essx-1C 6
Haroldswick. Shet-1H 37
Harpenden. Hert-1B 6
Harrogate. N.Yk-4D 20
Harrow. G.Ln-2B 6
Hartburn. Nmbd-4G 25
Hartfield. E.Su-4C 6
Harthill. Stra-1H 23
Hartington. Derb-3B 16
Hartland. Devn-2E 3
Hartlebury. H&W-2D 10
Hartlepool. Clev-1D 20
Hartley. Wintney. Hamp
  -3A 6
Hartpury. Glos-4D 10
Hartshill. War-1F 11
Harvington. H&W-3E 11
Harwell. Oxfd-5F 11
Harwich. Essx-5G 13
Harworth. Nott-2D 16
Haslemere. Surr-4A 6
Haslingden. Lanc-1H 15
Hastings. E.Su-5E 7
Hatfield. Hert-1B 6
Hatfield. S.Yk-1D 16
Hatfield Heath. Essx-1D 6
Hatfield Woodhouse. S.Yk
  -1D 16
Hatherleigh. Devn-2F 3
Hathern. Leic-5C 16
Hathersage. Derb-2B 16
Hatton. Derb-4B 16
Hatton. Grmp-4H 33
Hatton of Fintray. Grmp
  -5G 33
Haugh of Urr. D&G-5H 23
Haughton. Staf-5H 15
Havant. Hamp-4G 5
Haverfordwest. Dyfd-4B 8
Haverhill. Suff-5D 12
Hawarden. Clwd-3F 15
Hawes. N.Yk-3H 19
Hawick. Bord-3E 25
Hawkhurst. Kent-4E 7
Hawkshead. Cumb-3F 19
Haworth. W.Yk-5C 20
Haxby. N.Yk-4E 21
Haxey. Humb-2E 17
Haydon Bridge. Nmbd
  -5F 25
Hayfield. Derb-2B 16
Hayle. Corn-5B 2
Hay-on-Wye. Powy-3G 9
Haywards Heath. W.Su
  -4C 6
Hazel Grove. G.Mn-2H 15
Heacham. Norf-1D 12
Headcorn. Kent-4E 7
Headley. Hamp-4A 6
Healing. Humb-1F 17
Heanor. Derb-4C 16
Heast. High-4E 31
Heathfield. E.Su-5D 6
Hebden Bridge. W.Yk
  -5H 19
Heckington. Linc-1B 12
Heddon-on-the-Wall.
  Nmbd-5G 25
Hedon. Humb-5G 21
Heighington. Dur-2C 20
Heiton. Bord-2E 25
Helensburgh. Stra-5B 28
Hellifield. N.Yk-4H 19
Helmsdale. High-1D 32
Helmsley. N.Yk-3E 21
Helpringham. Linc-1B 12
Helpston. Camb-2B 12
Helsby. Ches-2F 15
Helston. Corn-5B 2
Hemel Hempstead. Hert
  -1B 6
Hemingborough. N.Yk
  -5E 21
Hemsby. Norf-2G 13
Hemsworth. W.Yk-1C 16
Hemyock. Devn-4A 4

Henfield. W.Su-5B 6
Henley-in-Arden. War
  -2E 11
Henley-on-Thames. Oxfd
  -2A 6
Henllan. Clwd-3E 15
Hereford. H&W-3H 9
Herne Bay. Kent-3F 7
Herstmonceux. E.Su-5D 6
Hertford. Hert-1C 6
Hessle. Humb-5G 21
Hest Bank. Lanc-4F 19
Heswall. Mers-2F 15
Hethersett. Norf-2F 13
Hetton-le-Hole. T&W
  -1D 20
Hexham. Nmbd-5F 25
Heysham. Lanc-4F 19
Heywood. G.Mn-1H 15
Hibaldstow. Humb-1E 17
Higham Ferrers. Nptn
  -4A 12
Highampton. Devn-2E 3
High Bentham. N.Yk-4H 19
Highbridge. Som-3B 4
High Dougarie. Stra-2D 22
High Eggborough. N.Yk
  -1D 16
High Ercall. Shrp-5G 15
High Etherley. Dur-1C 20
Highley. Shrp-1C 10
Hightae. D&G-4C 24
Highworth. Wilt-5E 11
High Wycombe. Buck-2A 6
Hildenborough. Kent-4D 6
Hilderstone. Staf-4H 15
Hilgay. Norf-3D 12
Hill of Fearn. High-2C 32
Hillside. Shet-3G 37
Hillside. Tays-2G 29
Hillswick. Shet-2G 37
Hilton. Derb-4B 16
Hilton of Cadboll. High
  -2C 32
Hinckley. Leic-1F 11
Hinderwell. N.Yk-2F 21
Hindhead. Surr-4A 6
Hindley. G.Mn-1G 15
Hindon. Wilt-3D 4
Hingham. Norf-2F 13
Hinstock. Shrp-4G 15
Hirwaun. M.Gl-4F 9
Histon. Camb-4C 12
Hitchin. Hert-5B 12
Hixon. Staf-5B 16
Hockley. Essx-2E 7
Hockley Heath. W.Md
  -2E 11
Hockliffe. Beds-5A 12
Hockwold cum Wilton.
  Norf-3D 12
Hoddesdon. Hert-1C 6
Hodnet. Shrp-4G 15
Hogsthorpe. Linc-3H 17
Holbeach. Linc-1C 12
Holbrook. Suff-5F 13
Holford. Som-3A 4
Holland. Orkn-1B 36
  (on Papa Westray)
Hollandstoun. Orkn-1D 36
Hollingbourne. Kent-3E 7
Hollym. Humb-1G 17
Hollywood. H&W-1E 11
Holme. Camb-3B 12
Holme next the Sea. Norf
  -1D 12
Holme-on-Spalding-Moor.
  Humb-5F 21
Holmes Chapel. Ches
  -3H 15
Holmfirth. W.Yk-1B 16
Holsworthy. Devn-2E 3
Holt. Clwd-3F 15
Holt. Norf-1F 13
Holt. Wilt-2D 4
Holton le Clay. Linc-1G 17
Holyhead. Gwyn-2A 14
Holywell. Clwd-3E 15
Holywood. D&G-4H 23
Honiton. Devn-4A 4
Honley. W.Yk-1B 16
Hook. Hamp-2G 5

Llanfair Talhaiarn. Clwd
-3D 14
Llanfechain. Powy-5E 15
Llanfihangel Rhydithon.
Powy-2G 9
Llanfrynach. Powy-3G 9
Llanfyllin. Powy-5E 15
Llanfyrnach. Dyfd-3C 8
Llangadfan. Powy-5E 15
Llangadog. Dyfd-3E 9
Llangefni. Gwyn-2B 14
Llangeitho. Dyfd-2E 9
Llangernyw. Clwd-3D 14
Llanglydwen. Dyfd-3C 8
Llangoed. Gwyn-2C 14
Llangollen. Clwd-4E 15
Llangorse. Powy-3G 9
Llangranog. Dyfd-2D 8
Llangunllo. Powy-2G 9
Llangurig. Powy-1F 9
Llangynidr. Powy-4G 9
Llangynog. Powy-4E 15
Llanidloes. Powy-1F 9
Llanilar. Dyfd-2E 9
Llanmadoc. W.Gl-5D 8
Llanon. Dyfd-2E 9
Llanpumsaint. Dyfd-3D 8
Llanrhaeadr-ym-Mochnant.
Clwd-4E 15
Llanrhystud. Dyfd-2E 9
Llanrug. Gwyn-3C 14
Llanrwst. Gwyn-3D 14
Llansanffraid Glan Conwy.
Gwyn-2D 14
Llansannan. Clwd-3D 14
Llansawel. Dyfd-3E 9
Llanstephan. Dyfd-4D 8
Llantrisant. M.Gl-5G 9
Llantwit Major. S.Gl-2A 4
Llanuwchllyn. Gwyn-4D 14
Llanwddyn. Powy-5E 15
Llanwnen. Dyfd-3E 9
Llanwnog. Powy-1G 9
Llanwrda. Dyfd-3E 9
Llanwrtyd Wells. Powy
-3F 9
Llanybyther. Dyfd-3E 9
Llanycefn. Dyfd-3C 8
Llanymynech. Powy &
Shrp-5F 15
Llay. Clwd-3F 15
Lledrod. Dyfd-2E 9
Llithfaen. Gwyn-4B 14
Llowes. Powy-3G 9
Llwyngwril. Gwyn-5C 14
Llynclys. Shrp-5F 15
Llyswen. Powy-3G 9
Loanhead. Loth-1D 24
Lochailort. High-1E 27
Lochaline. High-3D 26
Lochans. D&G-5E 23
Lochawe. Stra-3F 27
Lochboisdale. W.Is-4B 30
Lochcarron. High-3F 31
Lochearnhead. Cent-4C 28
Locheport. W.Is-2B 30
Lochgair. Stra-3F 27
Lochgelly. Fife-5E 29
Lochgilphead. Stra-5E 27
Lochgoilhead. Stra-4F 27
Lochinver. High-3E 35
Lochmaben. D&G-4C 24
Lochportain. W.Is-2B 30
Lochranza. Stra-1D 22
Lochskipport. W.Is-3B 30
Lochwinnoch. Stra-1F 23
Lockerbie. D&G-4C 24
Lockton. N.Yk-3F 21
Loddon. Norf-3G 13
Loftus. Clev-2E 21
Logie Coldstone. Grmp
-5E 33
London. G.Ln-2C 6
Long Bennington. Linc
-1A 12
Longbridge Deverill. Wilt
-3D 4
Long Buckby. Nptn-2G 11
Long Compton. War-3F 11
Long Eaton. Derb-4C 16
Longforgan. Tays-3F 29

Longframlington. Nmbd
-3G 25
Long Hanborough. Oxfd
-4F 11
Longhope. Orkn-3B 36
Longhorsley. Nmbd-4G 25
Longhoughton. Nmbd
-3G 25
Long Itchington. War
-2F 11
Long Lawford. War-1F 11
Longmanhill. Grmp-3F 33
Long Marston. N.Yk-4D 20
Long Melford. Suff-5E 13
Longmorn. Grmp-3D 32
Longnewton. Clev-2D 20
Longniddry. Loth-5F 29
Longnor. Staf-3B 16
Long Preston. N.Yk-4H 19
Longridge. Lanc-5G 19
Longside. Grmp-4H 33
Longstanton. Camb-4C 12
Long Stratton. Norf-3F 13
Long Sutton. Linc-2E 12
Longton. Lanc-5F 19
Longton. Staf-4H 15
Longtown. Cumb-5D 24
Looe. Corn-4E 3
Loppington. Shrp-4F 15
Lossiemouth. Grmp-3D 32
Lostwithiel. Corn-4D 2
Loughborough. Leic-5D 16
Loughor. W.Gl-5F 9
Loughton. Essx-2C 6
Louth. Linc-2G 17
Lowdham. Nott-4D 16
Low Eggborough. N.Yk
-4G 15
Lower Diabaig. High-2F 31
Lower Killeyan. Stra-2B 22
Lower Ollach. High-3E 31
Lowestoft. Suff-3H 13
Lowick. Nmbd-2G 25
Ludag. W.Is-4B 30
Ludborough. Linc-2G 17
Ludford. Linc-2F 17
Ludgershall. Wilt-2F 5
Ludham. Norf-2G 13
Ludlow. Shrp-2C 10
Lumphanan. Grmp-5F 33
Luncarty. Tays-3E 29
Luss. Stra-5B 28
Lusta. High-2D 30
Luton. Beds-1B 6
Lutterworth. Leic-1G 11
Lydbury North. Shrp-1H 9
Lydd. Kent-5F 7
Lydiate. Mers-1F 15
Lydney. Glos-4C 10
Lyme Regis. Dors-5B 4
Lyminge. Kent-4F 7
Lymington. Hamp-5F 5
Lymm. Ches-2G 15
Lyndhurst. Hamp-4F 5
Lyneham. Wilt-5E 11
Lynemouth. Nmbd-4H 25
Lyness. Orkn-3B 36
Lyng. Som-3B 4
Lynton. Devn-1F 3
Lytchett Minster. Dors
-5D 4
Lytham. Lanc-5F 19
Lytham St Anne's. Lanc
-5F 19

Mablethorpe. Linc-2H 17
Macclesfield. Ches-3H 15
Macduff. Grmp-3F 33
Macharioch. Stra-3C 22
Machrihanish. Stra-3C 22
Machynlleth. Powy-5C 14
Madeley. Shrp-5G 15
Madeley. Staf-4H 15
Madley. H&W-3H 9
Maentwrog. Gwyn-4C 14
Maesteg. M.Gl-5F 9
Maghull. Mers-1F 15
Magor. Gwnt-5H 9
Maiden Bradley. Wilt-3D 4
Maidenhead. Berk-2A 5

Maiden Newton. Dors-5C 4
Maidens. Stra-3E 23
Maidstone. Kent-3D 6
Maldon. Essx-1E 7
Mallaig. High-1D 26
Mallwyd. Gwyn-5D 14
Malmesbury. Wilt-5D 10
Malpas. Ches-4F 15
Maltby. S.Yk-2D 16
Maltby le Marsh. Linc
-2G 17
Malton. N.Yk-4F 21
Manby. Linc-2G 17
Manchester. G.Mn-2H 15
Manea. Camb-2D 12
Mangotsfield. Avon-5C 10
Manish. W.Is-1C 30
Manningtree. Essx-5F 13
Manorbier. Dyfd-5C 8
Mansfield. Nott-3D 16
Mansfield Woodhouse.
Nott-3D 16
March. Camb-3C 12
Marcham. Oxfd-5F 11
Marchington. Staf-4B 16
Marchwiel. Clwd-4F 15
Marden. Kent-4D 6
Mareham le Fen. Linc
-3G 17
Margate. Kent-3G 7
Mark. Som-3B 4
Market Bosworth. Leic
-5C 16
Market Deeping. Linc
-2B 12
Market Drayton. Shrp
-4G 15
Market Harborough. Leic
-1G 11
Market Lavington. Wilt
-2E 5
Market Rasen. Linc-2F 17
Market Weighton. Humb
-5F 21
Markfield. Leic-5C 16
Marksbury. Avon-2C 4
Markyate. Hert-1B 6
Marlborough. Wilt-2E 5
Marloes. Dyfd-4B 8
Marlow. Buck-2A 6
Marple. G.Mn-2H 15
Marsden. W.Yk-1B 16
Marshfield. Avon-2D 4
Marske-by-the-Sea. Clev
-2E 21
Marston Magna. Som-4C 4
Martham. Norf-2G 13
Martlesham Heath. Suff
-5F 13
Martley. H&W-2C 10
Martock. Som-4B 4
Marton. Linc-2E 17
Marvig. W.Is-3B 34
Marybank. High-3A 32
(nr. Dingwall)
Marykirk. Grmp-2G 29
Maryport. Cumb-1E 19
Masham. N.Yk-3C 20
Mathry. Dyfd-3B 8
Matlock. Derb-3C 16
Mauchline. Stra-2F 23
Maud. Grmp-4G 33
Mawbray. Cumb-1E 19
Maxwellheugh. Bord-2E 25
Maybole. Stra-3F 23
Mayfield. Staf-4B 16
Mealsgate. Cumb-1E 19
Meare. Som-3B 4
Measham. Leic-5C 16
Meavaig. W.Is-3A 34
Medbourne. Leic-3A 12
Medstead. Hamp-3G 5
Meidrim. Dyfd-4D 8
Meifod. Powy-5E 15
Meigle. Tays-3F 29
Meikle Wartle. Grmp-4F 33
Melbost. W.Is-2B 34
Melbourn. Camb-5C 12
Melbourne. Derb-5C 16
Melby. Shet-3F 37
Melksham. Wilt-2D 4
Mellon Charles. High-1F 31

Mellon Udrigle. High-1F 31
Mellor. Lanc-5G 19
Melmerby. Cumb-1G 19
Melrose. Bord-2E 25
Meltham. W.Yk-1B 16
Melton Mowbray. Leic
-2A 12
Melvaig. High-1E 31
Melvich. High-1H 35
Memsie. Grmp-3G 33
Menai Bridge. Gwyn-3C 14
Mennock. D&G-3H 23
Menston. W.Yk-5C 20
Meonstoke. Hamp-4G 5
Meopham. Kent-3D 6
Mere. Wilt-3D 4
Meriden. W.Md-1E 11
Merriott. Som-4B 4
Merthyr Cynog. Powy-3F 9
Merthyr Tydfil. M.Gl-4G 9
Merton. G.Ln-3C 6
Messingham. Humb-1E 17
Metfield. Suff-3F 13
Metheringham. Linc-3F 17
Methil. Fife-5F 29
Methlick. Grmp-4G 33
Methven. Tays-3E 29
Methwold. Norf-3D 12
Mevagissey. Corn-5D 2
Mexborough. S.Yk-1C 16
Miavaig. W.Is-2A 34
Mickleton. Glos-3E 11
Midbea. Orkn-1B 36
Middle Barton. Oxfd-3F 11
Middleham. N.Yk-3C 20
Middlesbrough. Clev
-2D 20
Middleton. G.Mn-1H 15
Middleton Cheney. Nptn
-3F 11
Middleton in Teesdale. Dur
-1H 19
Middleton St George. Dur
-2D 20
Middle Wallop. Hamp-3F 5
Middlewich. Ches-3G 15
Midhurst. W.Su-5A 6
Midsomer Norton. Avon
-2C 4
Mid Yell. Shet-2H 37
Migvie. Grmp-5E 33
Milborne Port. Som-4C 4
Mildenhall. Suff-4D 12
Milfield. Nmbd-2F 25
Milford Haven. Dyfd-4B 8
Milford on Sea. Hamp-5F 5
Millbrook. Corn-4E 3
Millom. Cumb-3E 19
Millport. Stra-1E 23
Milltown. Grmp-4F 33
(nr. Huntly)
Milltown. High-3A 32
Milngavie. Stra-1G 23
Milnrow. G.Mn-1H 15
Milnthorpe. Cumb-3F 19
Milovaig. High-3C 30
Milton. Camb-4C 12
Milton. Dyfd-4C 8
Milton Abbot. Devn-3E 3
Milton Keynes. Buck-5A 12
Milton of Campsie. Stra
-5C 28
Milverton. Som-3A 4
Milwich. Staf-4H 15
Minard. Stra-5F 27
Mindrum. Nmbd-2F 25
Minehead. Som-1G 3
Minnigaff. D&G-5F 23
Minster. Kent-3G 7
(nr. Ramsgate)
Minster. Kent-3E 7
(nr. Sheerness)
Minsterley. Shrp-5F 15
Mintlaw. Grmp-4H 33
Mirfield. W.Yk-1B 16
Misterton. Nott-2E 17
Mitcheldean. Glos-4C 10
Mitford. Nmbd-4G 25
Mochrum. D&G-1B 18
Modbury. Devn-4G 3
Moelfre. Gwyn-2C 14
Moffat. D&G-3C 24
Mold. Clwd-3E 15

Moniaive. D&G-4H 23
Monifieth. Tays-3G 29
Monkland. H&W-2H 9
Monks Eleigh. Suff-5E 13
Monmouth. Gwnt-4H 9
Montgomery. Powy-1G 9
Montrose. Tays-2G 29
Monymusk. Grmp-5F 33
Morar. High-1D 26
Morcott. Leic-2A 12
Mordiford. H&W-3C 10
Morebattle. Bord-3F 25
Morecambe. Lanc-4F 19
Moretonhampstead. Devn
-3G 3
Moreton-in-Marsh. Glos
-3E 11
Morfa Nefyn. Gwyn-4B 14
Morley. W.Yk-5D 20
Morpeth. Nmbd-4G 25
Morriston. W.Gl-5E 9
Mortimer's Cross. H&W
-2H 9
Morton. Linc-2B 12
Morville. Shrp-1C 10
Morwenstow. Corn-2D 2
Mossblown. Stra-3F 23
Mossley. G.Mn-1H 15
Mostyn. Clwd-2E 15
Motherwell. Stra-1H 23
Moulin. Tays-2D 28
Moulton. Linc-2C 12
Moulton. Suff-4D 12
Mountain Ash. M.Gl-5G 9
Mountsorrel. Leic-5D 16
Mousehole. Corn-5A 2
Mouswald. D&G-5C 24
Mow Cop. Ches & Staf
-3H 15
Moylgrove. Dyfd-3C 8
Muasdale. Stra-2C 22
Much Marcle. H&W-3C 10
Much Wenlock. Shrp
-5G 15
Muie. High-3G 35
Muirdrum. Tays-3G 29
Muirhead. Stra-1G 23
Muirhead. Tays-3F 29
Muirkirk. Stra-2G 23
Muir of Ord. High-4B 32
Mulbarton. Norf-2F 13
Mulben. Grmp-3E 33
Mumbles, The. W.Gl-5E 9
Mumby. Linc-3H 17
Mundesley. Norf-1G 13
Munlochy. High-3B 32
Murthly. Tays-3E 29
Murton. Dur-1D 20
Musselburgh. Loth-1D 24
Muthill. Tays-4D 28
Mybster. High-4A 36
Mynytho. Gwyn-4B 14
Mytholmroyd. W.Yk-5C 20

Naast. High-1F 31
Nailsea. Avon-2B 4
Nailsworth. Glos-5D 10
Nairn. High-3C 32
Nantgaredig. Dyfd-4D 8
Nantwich. Ches-4G 15
Narberth. Dyfd-4C 8
Narborough. Leic-1G 11
Narborough. Norf-2D 12
Naseby. Nptn-1G 11
Navenby. Linc-3E 17
Nayland. Suff-5E 13
Neath. W.Gl-5F 9
Necton. Norf-2E 13
Needham Market. Suff
-4F 13
Needingworth. Camb
-4C 12
Nefyn. Gwyn-4B 14
Neilston. Stra-1F 23
Nelson. Lanc-5H 19
Nenthorn. Bord-2E 25
Neston. Ches-2E 15
Netheravon. Wilt-3E 5
Nether Broughton. Leic
-4D 16
Nether Poppleton. N.Yk
-4E 21
Nether Stowey. Som-3A 4
Netherton. Tays-2G 29
(nr. Brechin)
Nethy Bridge. High-5D 32
Nettleham. Linc-3F 17
New Abbey. D&G-5H 23
New Aberdour. Grmp
-3G 33
New Alresford. Hamp-3G 5
Newark-on-Trent. Nott
-3E 17
Newbiggin-by-the-Sea.
Nmbd-4H 25
Newbigging. Tays-3F 29
(nr. Monikie)
Newbold Verdon. Leic
-5C 16
Newborough. Camb-2B 12
Newbridge on Wye. Powy
-2G 9
Newburgh. Grmp-4G 33
Newbury. Berk-2F 5
Newby Bridge. Cumb
-3F 19
New Byth. Grmp-3G 33
Newcastle. Shrp-1G 9
Newcastle Emlyn. Dyfd
-3D 8
Newcastleton. Bord-4D 24
Newcastle-under-Lyme.
Staf-4H 15
Newcastle upon Tyne.
T&W-5G 25
New Cumnock. Stra-3G 23
New Deer. Grmp-4G 33
New Elgin. Grmp-3D 32
Newent. Glos-3C 10
New Galloway. D&G-4G 23
Newhaven. E.Su-5C 6
New Holland. Humb-1F 17
Newick. E.Su-5C 6
New Leeds. Grmp-3H 33
New Luce. D&G-5E 23
Newlyn. Corn-5A 2
Newmachar. Grmp-5G 33
Newmarket. Suff-4D 12
Newmarket. W.Is-2B 34
Newmill. Grmp-3E 33
(nr. Keith)
New Mills. Derb-2B 16
Newmilns. Stra-2G 23
New Milton. Hamp-5E 5
Newnham. Glos-4C 10
Newnham. Nptn-2G 11
New Pitsligo. Grmp-3G 33
Newport. Dyfd-3C 8
Newport. Gwnt-5H 9
Newport. IOW-5G 5
Newport. Shrp-5G 15
Newport-on-Tay. Fife
-3F 29
Newport Pagnell. Buck
-5A 12
Newquay. Corn-4C 2
New Quay. Dyfd-2D 8
New Radnor. Powy-2G 9
New Romney. Kent-4F 7
New Rossington. S.Yk
-2D 16
New Scone. Tays-3E 29
Newton. D&G-5D 24
(nr. Annan)
Newton. D&G-4C 24
(nr. Moffat)
Newton. Stra-5F 27
(nr. Strachur)
Newton Aycliffe. Dur-2D 20
Newton Ferrers. Devn-5F 3
Newtonferry. W.Is-1B 30
Newtongrange. Loth-1D 24
Newtonhill. Grmp-1H 29
Newton-le-Willows. Mers
-2G 15
Newtonmore. High-1C 29
Newton on Trent. Linc
-3E 17

Newton Stewart-Sale

Newton Stewart. D&G -5F 23
Newtown. Powy-1G 9
Newtown St Boswells. Bord-2E 25
New Tredegar. M.Gl-4G 9
Newtyle. Tays-3F 29
New Waltham. Humb -1G 17
Nigg. High-3C 32
Nigg Ferry. High-3C 32
Ninemile Bar. D&G-5H 23
Ninfield. E.Su-5D 6
Niwbwrch. Gwyn-3B 14
Normanton. W.Yk-1C 16
Northallerton. N.Yk-3D 20
Northam. Devn-1E 3
Northampton. Nptn-4A 12
North Anston. S.Yk-2D 16
North Ballachulish. High -2F 27
North Berwick. Loth-5G 29
North Cave. Humb-5F 21
Northchapel. W.Su-4A 6
North Collingham. Nott -3E 17
North Dalton. Humb-4F 21
North Elmham. Norf-2E 13
North Erradale. High-1E 31
Northfleet. Kent-3D 6
North Hykeham. Linc -3E 17
Northiam. E.Su-4E 7
North Kelsey. Linc-1F 17
North Kessock. High-4B 32
North Kilworth. Leic-1G 11
North Molton. Devn-1F 3
North Newbald. Humb -5F 21
North Petherton. Som-3B 4
North Roe. Shet-2E 33
North Shields. T&W-5H 25
North Somercotes. Linc -2G 17
North Tidworth. Wilt-3E 5
North Tolsta. W.Is-2C 34
Northton. W.Is-1B 30
North Walsham. Norf -1G 13
North Weald Bassett. Essx -1C 6
Northwich. Ches-3G 15
Northwingfield. Derb -3C 16
Northwold. Norf-3D 12
Northwood. D.Ln-2B 6
Norton. Gwnt-4H 9
Norton. N.Yk-4F 21
Norton. Powy-2H 9
Norton Fitzwarren. Som -3A 4
Norwich. Norf-2F 13
Nottingham. Nott-1D 16
Nuneaton. War-1F 11
Nybster. High-4B 36

Oadby. Leic-5D 16
Oakengates. Shrp-5G 15
Oakham. Leic-2A 12
Oakley. Fife-5E 29
Oban. Stra-3E 27
Ochiltree. Stra-3G 23
Oddsta. Shet-2H 37
Ogmore-by-Sea. M.Gl-5F 9
Okehampton. Devn-3F 3
Oldbury. W.Md-1D 10
Old Deer. Grmp-4G 33
Old Fletton. Camb-3B 12
Oldham. G.Mn-1H 15
Old Leake. Linc-3G 17
Oldmeldrum. Grmp-4G 33
Oldshoremore. High-1E 35
Old Windsor. Berk-3A 6
Ollaberry. Shet-2G 37
Ollerton. Nott-3D 16
Olney. Buck-4A 12
Ombersley. H&W-2D 10
Opinan. High-2E 31
  (nr. Gairloch)
Orford. Suff-4G 13
Orleton. H&W-2H 9

Ormesby St Margaret. Norf -2G 13
Ormiston. Loth-1D 24
Ormskirk. Lanc-1F 15
Orpington. G.Ln-3C 6
Orrell. G.Mn-1G 15
Orton. Cumb-2G 19
Osbournby. Linc-1B 12
Osmington. Dors-5C 4
Osmotherley. N.Yk-3D 20
Ossett. W.Yk-1C 16
Oswaldkirk. N.Yk-3E 21
Oswaldtwistle. Lanc-5G 19
Oswestry. Shrp-4F 15
Othery. Som-3B 4
Otley. W.Yk-5C 20
Otterburn. Nmbd-4F 25
Otter Ferry. Stra-5E 27
Ottery St Mary. Devn-5A 4
Oundle. Nptn-3B 12
Outwell. Norf-2D 12
Overbiste. Orkn-1C 36
Overseal. Derb-5C 16
Overstrand. Norf-1F 13
Overton. Clwd-4F 15
Overton. Hamp-3B 6
Oxenhope. W.Yk-5C 20
Oxford. Oxfd-4G 11
Oxted. Surr-3C 6
Oxton. Bord-1F 24
Oykel Bridge. High-3F 35
Oyne. Grmp-4F 33

Pabail Uarach. W.Is-2C 34
Padbury. Buck-3G 11
Paddock Wood. Kent-4D 6
Padiham. Lanc-5H 19
Padstow. Corn-4C 2
Paignton. Devn-4G 3
Painshawfield. Nmbd -5G 25
Painswick. Glos-4D 10
Paisley. Stra-1F 23
Palnackie. D&G-5H 23
Palnure. D&G-5F 23
Pandy. Gwnt-4H 9
Pandy. Gwyn-4D 14
Pangbourne. Berk-5G 11
Pant. Shrp-5F 15
Papworth Everard. Camb -4C 12
Parkeston. Essx-5F 13
Parkgate. D&G-4C 24
Parracombe. Devn-1F 3
Partington. G.Mn-2G 15
Partney. Linc-3G 17
Parton. D&G-5G 23
Patchway. Avon-5C 10
Pateley Bridge. N.Yk-4C 20
Pathhead. Loth-1D 24
Patna. Stra-3F 23
Patrington. Humb-1G 17
Pattingham. Staf-1D 10
Paulton. Avon-2C 4
Paxton. Bord-1F 25
Peacehaven. E.Su-5C 6
Peasedown St John. Avon -2C 4
Peebles. Bord-2D 24
Peel. IOM-3A 18
Pegswood. Nmbd-4G 25
Peinchorran. High-3E 31
Pembrey. Dyfd-4D 8
Pembroke. Dyfd-4B 8
Pembroke Dock. Dyfd-4B 8
Pembury. Kent-4D 6
Penally. Dyfd-5C 8
Penarth. S.Gl-2A 4
Pencader. Dyfd-3D 8
Pencoed. M.Gl-5F 9
Penderyn. M.Gl-4F 9
Pendine. Dyfd-4C 8
Penicuik. Loth-1C 24
Penistone. S.Yk-1B 16
Penkridge. Staf-5H 15
Penley. Clwd-4F 15
Penmachno. Gwyn-3D 14
Penmaenmawr. Gwyn -2C 14
Pennan. Grmp-3G 33
Penpont. D&G-4H 23

Penrhyn Bay. Gwyn-2D 14
Penrhyndeudraeth. Gwyn -4C 14
Penrith. Cumb-1G 19
Penruddock. Cumb-1F 19
Penryn. Corn-5C 2
Pensford. Avon-2C 4
Penshurst. Kent-4D 6
Pentraeth. Gwyn-2C 14
Pentrefoelas. Clwd-3D 14
Pen-y-groes. Dyfd-4E 9
Penygroes. Gwyn-3B 14
Penzance. Corn-5A 2
Perranporth. Corn-4C 2
Pershore. H&W-3D 10
Perth. Tays-4E 29
Peterborough. Camb -3B 12
Peterculter. Grmp-5G 33
Peterhead. Grmp-4H 33
Peterlee. Dur-1D 20
Petersfield. Hamp-5A 6
Peterstow. H&W-4C 10
Petworth. W.Su-5A 6
Pewsey. Wilt-2E 5
Pickering. N.Yk-3F 21
Piddletrenthide. Dors-4C 4
Pierowall. Orkn-1B 36
Pinchbeck. Linc-1B 12
Pinmore. Stra-4E 23
Pinwherry. Stra-4E 23
Pirnmill. Stra-2D 22
Pitlochry. Tays-2D 28
Pitmedden. Grmp-4G 33
Pitscottie. Fife-4F 29
Pitstone Green. Buck-1A 6
Pittenweem. Fife-4G 29
Plockton. High-3F 31
Pluckley. Kent-4E 7
Plumbland. Cumb-1E 19
Plumpton. Cumb-1G 19
Plymouth. Devn-4E 3
Plympton. Devn-4F 3
Plymstock. Devn-4F 3
Pocklington. Humb-5F 21
Polbain. High-3D 34
Polegate. E.Su-5D 6
Poleworth. War-5C 16
Polperro. Corn-4D 2
Polwarth. Bord-1F 25
Pontardawe. W.Gl-4E 9
Pontardulais. W.Gl-4E 9
Pontefract. W.Yk-1C 16
Ponteland. Nmbd-5G 25
Ponterwyd. Dyfd-1E 9
Pontesbury. Shrp-5F 15
Pontrhydfendigaid. Dyfd -2E 9
Pont-rhyd-y-groes. Dyfd -2E 9
Pontrilas. H&W-3H 9
Pontyates. Dyfd-4D 8
Pontyberem. Dyfd-4E 9
Pontyclun. M.Gl-5G 9
Pontycymer. M.Gl-5F 9
Pontypool. Gwnt-5H 9
Pontypridd. M.Gl-5G 9
Pool. W.Yk-5C 20
Poole. Dors-5E 5
Poolewe. High-1F 31
Poringland. Norf-2G 13
Porlock. Som-1G 3
Port Askaig. Stra-1B 22
Port Bannatyne. Stra-1E 23
Port Charlotte. Stra-1A 22
Portdinorwic. Gwyn-3C 14
Port Ellen. Stra-2B 22
Port Erin. IOM-4A 18
Portesham. Dors-5C 4
Port Eynon. W.Gl-5D 8
Port Glasgow. Stra-1F 23
Portgordon. Grmp-3E 33
Porth. M.Gl-5G 9
Porthcawl. M.Gl-5F 9
Porthleven. Corn-5B 2
Porthmadog. Gwyn-4C 14
Port Isaac. Corn-3C 2
Portishead. Avon-5H 9
Portknockie. Grmp-3E 33
Port Lamont. Stra-1E 23
Portlethen. Grmp-1H 29
Port Logan. D&G-1A 18

Portmahomack. High -2C 32
Portnacroish. Stra-3E 27
Portnahaven. Stra-1A 22
Portnalong. High-3D 30
Port nan Giuran. W.Is -2C 34
Port of Ness. W.Is-1C 34
Portpatrick. D&G-5D 22
Portreath. Corn-5B 2
Portree. High-3D 30
Port St Mary. IOM-4A 18
Portskerra. High-1H 35
Portsmouth. Hamp-4G 5
Portsoy. Grmp-3F 33
Port Talbot. W.Gl-5E 9
Port William. Bord-1B 6
Potters Bar. Hert-1B 6
Potterspury. Nptn-5A 12
Potterton. Grmp-5G 33
Potton. Beds-4B 12
Poulton-le-Fylde. Lanc -5F 19
Poynton. Ches-2H 15
Prees. Shrp-4G 15
Prescot. Mers-2F 15
Prestatyn. Clwd-2E 15
Prestbury. Ches-2H 15
Presteigne. Powy-2H 9
Preston. Bord-1F 25
Preston. Humb-5G 21
Preston. Lanc-5G 19
Preston Candover. Hamp -3G 5
Prestwick. Stra-3F 23
Prestwood. Buck-1A 6
Prickwillow. Camb-3D 12
Princes Risborough. Buck -1A 6
Princetown. Devn-4F 3
Probus. Corn-5C 2
Prudhoe. Nmbd-5G 25
Puddletown. Dors-5D 4
Pudsey. W.Yk-5C 20
Pulborough. W.Su-5B 6
Pulham Market. Norf-3F 13
Pumpsaint. Dyfd-3E 9
Purley. G.Ln-3C 6
Purton. Wilt-5E 11
Pwllheli. Gwyn-4B 14
Pyle. W.Gl-5F 9

Queenborough. Kent-3E 7
Queensbury. W.Yk-5C 20
Queensferry. Clwd-3F 15
Queniborough. Leic-5D 16
Quorndon. Leic-5D 16

Radcliffe. G.Mn-1H 15
Radcliffe on Trent. Nott -4D 16
Radlett. Hert-2B 6
Radstock. Avon-2C 4
Radyr. S.Gl-5G 9
Rafford. Grmp-3D 32
Raglan. Gwnt-4H 9
Rainford. Mers-1F 15
Rainham. Kent-3E 7
Rainworth. Nott-3D 16
Ramasaig. High-3C 30
Ramsbottom. G.Mn-1H 15
Ramsey. Camb-3B 12
Ramsey. IOM-3B 18
Ramsgate. Kent-3G 7
Ranish. W.Is-3B 34
Rankinston. Stra-3F 23
Ranskill. Nott-2D 16
Rathen. Grmp-3H 33
Rattray. Tays-3E 29
Raunds. Nptn-4B 12
Ravenshead. Nott-3D 16
Rawcliffe. Humb-1D 16
Rawmarsh. S.Yk-2C 16
Rawtenstall. Lanc-1H 15
Rayleigh. Essx-2E 7
Reading. Berk-2G 5
Rearquhar. High-2B 32
Reay. High-1H 35
Redbourn. Hert-1B 6
Redbourne. Humb-2E 17

Redcar. Clev-2E 21
Redcastle. High-4B 32
Redditch. H&W-2E 11
Redesdale Camp. Nmbd -4F 25
Redford. Tays-3G 29
Redhill. Surr-4C 6
Redpoint. High-2E 31
Red Roses. Dyfd-4C 8
Redruth. Corn-5B 2
Reedham. Norf-2G 13
Reepham. Norf-2F 13
Reeth. N.Yk-3C 20
Reigate. Surr-4C 6
Reighton. N.Yk-3G 21
Reiss. High-4B 36
Renfrew. Stra-1G 23
Rennington. Nmbd-3G 25
Repton. Derb-4C 16
Resolven. W.Gl-4F 9
Reston. Bord-1F 25
Reynoldston. W.Gl-5D 8
Rhandirmwyn. Dyfd-3F 9
Rhayader. Powy-2F 9
Rhiconich. High-1E 35
Rhoslanerchrugog. Clwd -4F 15
Rhosneigr. Gwyn-3B 14
Rhossili. W.Gl-5D 8
Rhosybol. Gwyn-2B 14
Rhu. Stra-5B 28
Rhuddlan. Clwd-2E 15
Rhyl. Clwd-2E 15
Rhymney. M.Gl-4G 9
Rhynie. Grmp-4E 33
Ribchester. Lanc-5G 19
Richmond. G.Ln-3B 6
Richmond. N.Yk-2C 20
Rieff. High-3D 34
Rievaulx. N.Yk-3E 21
Rigside. Stra-2H 23
Rillington. N.Yk-4F 21
Ringford. D&G-5G 23
Ringwood. Hamp-4E 5
Ripley. Derb-3C 16
Ripon. N.Yk-4D 20
Rippenden. W.Yk-1B 16
Risca. Gwnt-5G 9
Rishton. Lanc-5G 19
Roade. Nptn-4A 12
Roag. High-3D 30
Robertsbridge. E.Su-5D 6
Robin Hood's Bay. N.Yk -2F 21
Rocester. Staf-4B 16
Rochdale. G.Mn-1H 15
Roche. Corn-4C 2
Rochester. Kent-3D 6
Rochford. Essx-2E 7 .
Rockcliffe. D&G-5H 23
Rodel. W.Is-1C 30
Rogart. High-3G 35
Rolvenden. Kent-4E 7
Romford. G.Ln-2C 6
Romiley. G.Mn-2H 15
Romsey. Hamp-4F 5
Rookley. IOW-5G 5
Roos. Humb-5H 21
Rosehearty. Grmp-3G 33
Rosemarket. Dyfd-4B 8
Rosemarkie. High-3B 32
Rosemount. Tays-3E 29
Roseneath. Stra-5B 28
Rossendale. Lanc-1H 15
Rossett. Clwd-3F 15
Ross-on-Wye. H&W-4C 10
Rosyth. Fife-5E 29
Rothbury. Nmbd-3G 25
Rotherham. S.Yk-2C 16
Rothes. Grmp-4E 33
Rothesay. Stra-1E 23
Rothienorman. Grmp -4F 33
Rothley. Leic-5D 16
Rothwell. Nptn-3A 12
Rothwell. W.Yk-5D 20
Rottal. Tays-2F 29
Rottingdean. E.Su-5C 6
Roughton. Norf-1F 13
Rowlands Gill. T&W-5G 25
Royal Leamington Spa. War-2F 11

Royal Tunbridge Wells. Kent-4D 6
Royston. Hert-5C 12
Royston. S.Yk-1C 16
Royton. G.Mn-1H 15
Ruabon. Clwd-4F 15
Ruddington. Nott-4D 16
Rudston. Humb-4G 21
Rudyard. Staf-3H 15
Rufford. Lanc-1F 15
Rugby. War-1G 11
Rugeley. Staf-5B 16
Ruislip. G.Ln-2B 6
Rumney. S.Gl-5G 9
Runcorn. Ches-2G 15
Rushden. Nptn-4A 12
Ruskington. Linc-3F 17
Ruthin. Clwd-3E 15
Ruthwell. D&G-5C 24
Ruyton-XI-Towns. Shrp -5F 15
Ryde. IOW-5G 5
Rye. E.Su-5E 7
Ryhall. Leic-2B 12
Ryhill. W.Yk-1C 16
Ryhope. T&W-5H 25
Ryton. T&W-5G 25
Ryton-on-Dunsmore. War -2F 11

Sacriston. Dur-1C 20
Saddell. Stra-2D 22
Saddleworth. G.Mn-1H 15
Saffron Walden. Essx -5D 12
St Abbs. Bord-1F 25
St Agnes. Corn-4B 2
St Albans. Hert-1B 6
St Andrews. Fife-4G 29
St Ann's. D&G-4C 24
St Arvans. Gwnt-5C 10
St Asaph. Clwd-3E 15
St Austell. Corn-4D 2
St Bees. Cumb-2D 18
St Blazey. Corn-4D 2
St Boswells. Bord-2E 25
St Brides. Dyfd-4B 8
St Bride's Major. M.Gl-5F 9
St Clears. Dyfd-4D 8
St Cleer. Corn-4E 3
St Columb Major. Corn -4C 2
St Combs. Grmp-3H 33
St Cyrus. Grmp-2G 29
St David's. Dyfd-3B 8
St Dennis. Corn-4C 2
St Dogmaels. Dyfd-3C 8
St Fergus. Grmp-3H 33
St Fillans. Tays-4C 28
St Gennys. Corn-3D 2
St Germans. Corn-4E 3
St Harmon. Powy-2F 9
St Helens. Mers-2G 15
St Ishmael's. Dyfd-4B 8
St Issey. Corn-4C 2
St Ives. Camb-4C 12
St Ives. Corn-5B 2
St John's. IOM-3B 18
St John's Chapel. Dur -1H 19
St John's Town of Dalry. D&G-4G 23
St Just. Corn-5A 2
St Madoes. Tays-4E 29
St Margaret's at Cliffe. Kent -4G 7
St Margaret's Hope. Orkn -3B 36
St Martin's. Shrp-4F 15
St Mary's. Orkn-2B 36
St Mary's Bay. Kent-4F 7
St Mawes. Corn-5C 2
St Mawgan. Corn-4C 2
St Minver. Corn-3C 2
St Monance. Fife-4G 29
St Neot. Corn-4D 2
St Neots. Camb-4B 12
St Osyth. Essx-1F 7
St Weonards. H&W-4H 9
Salcombe. Devn-5F 3

Salen. High-2D 26
Salen. Stra-3D 26
Salford. G.Mn-2H 15
Saline. Fife-5E 29
Salisbury. Wilt-3E 5
Sallachy. High-3F 31
(nr. Darnie)
Saltash. Corn-4E 3
Saltburn-by-the-Sea. Clev
-2E 21
Saltcoats. Stra-2E 23
Saltfleet. Linc-2G 17
Samala. W.Is-2B 30
Sanaigmore. Stra-1A 22
Sandbach. Ches-3G 15
Sandbank. Stra-5F 27
Sandhaven. Grmp-3G 33
Sandhead. D&G-1A 18
Sandhurst. Berk-3A 6
Sandown. IOW-5G 5
Sandplace. Corn-4E 3
Sandringham. Norf-1D 12
Sandsend. N.Yk-2F 21
Sandwich. Kent-3G 7
Sandwick. W.Is-3B 30
(on South Uist)
Sandy. Beds-4B 12
Sanquhar. D&G-3H 23
Sapcote. Leic-1F 11
Sarclet. High-5B 36
Sarre. Kent-3G 7
Sauchen. Grmp-5F 33
Saul. Glos-4D 10
Saundersfoot. Dyfd-4C 8
Sawbridgeworth. Hert-1C 6
Sawston. Camb-5C 12
Sawtry. Camb-3B 12
Saxilby. Linc-2E 17
Saxmundham. Suff-4G 13
Saxthorpe. Norf-1F 13
Scalasaig. Stra-5C 26
Scalby. N.Yk-3F 21
Scalloway. Shet-4G 37
Scamblesby. Linc-2G 17
Scarborough. N.Yk-3G 21
Scardroy. High-2G 31
Scarfskerry. High-3B 36
Scarinish. Stra-3B 26
Scarisbrick. Lanc-1F 15
Scartho. Humb-1G 17
Scawby. Humb-1E 17
Scole. Norf-3F 13
Sconser. High-3E 31
Scotby. Cumb-5D 24
Scotch Corner. N.Yk-2C 20
Scotter. Linc-1E 17
Scourie. High-3F 35
Scousburgh. Shet-5G 37
Scrabster. High-3A 36
Scunthorpe. Humb-1E 17
Seaford. E.Su-5C 6
Seaham. Dur-1D 20
Seahouses. Nmbd-2G 25
Seamill. Stra-2E 23
Seascale. Cumb-2E 19
Seaton. Devn-5A 4
Seaton Carew. Clev-1E 21
Seaton Delaval. Nmbd
-4H 25
Seaview. IOW-5G 5
Sedbergh. Cumb-3G 19
Sedgefield. Dur-2C 20
Sedgley. W.Md-1D 10
Seend. Wilt-2D 4
Selattyn. Shrp-4F 15
Selborne. Hamp-3G 5
Selby. N.Yk-5E 21
Selkirk. Bord-2E 25
Sellafirth. Shet-2H 37
Selsey. W.Su-5H 5
Sennen. Corn-5A 2
Sennybridge. Powy-3F 9
Settle. N.Yk-3H 19
Sevenoaks. Kent-3D 6
Shader. W.Is-1B 34
Shaftesbury. Dors-4D 4
Shandon. Stra-5B 28
Shanklin. IOW-5G 5
Shap. Cumb-2G 19
Sharnford. Leic-1F 11
Shavington. Ches-3G 15
Shaw. G.Mn-1H 15

Shawbost. W.Is-2A 34
Shawbury. Shrp-5G 15
Shawhead. D&G-4H 23
Shebster. High-4A 36
Sheerness. Kent-3E 7
Sheffield. S.Yk-2C 16
Shefford. Beds-5B 12
Shelf. W.Yk-5C 20
Shenstone. Staf-5B 16
Shepshed. Leic-5C 16
Shepton Mallet. Som-3C 4
Sherborne. Dors-4C 4
Sherburn. N.Yk-3F 21
Sherburn in Elmet. N.Yk
-5D 20
Sheringham. Norf-1F 13
Sherston. Wilt-5D 10
Shiel Bridge. High-4F 31
(nr. Loch Shieldaig)
Shifnal. Shrp-5G 15
Shilbottle. Nmbd-3G 25
Shildon. Dur-1C 20
Shinness. High-3G 35
Shipdham. Norf-2E 13
Shipley. W.Yk-5C 20
Shipston on Stour. War
-3F 11
Shipton-under-Wychwood.
Oxfd-4F 11
Shirebrook. Derb-3D 16
Shirenewton. Gwnt-5H 9
Shobdon. H&W-2H 9
Shoeburyness. Essx-2E 7
Shoreham-by-Sea. W.Su
-4B 4
Shotley Gate. Suff-5F 13
Shotts. Stra-1H 23
Shrewsbury. Shrp-5F 15
Shrewton. Wilt-3E 5
Shrivenham. Oxfd-5E 11
Shulishader. W.Is-2C 34
Sible Hedingham. Essx
-5E 13
Sibsey. Linc-3G 17
Sidbury. Devn-5A 4
Sidmouth. Devn-5A 4
Sigglesthorne. Humb
-5G 21
Sileby. Leic-5D 16
Silloth. Cumb-5C 24
Silsden. W.Yk-5C 20
Silverstone. Nptn-3G 11
Simonsbath. Som-1G 3
Singleton. W.Su-5A 6
Sittingbourne. Kent-3E 7
Sixpenny Handley. Dors
-4D 4
Skaill. Orkn-2C 36
(nr. Deerness)
Skares. Stra-3G 23
Skeffling. Humb-1G 17
Skegness. Linc-3H 17
Skellingthorpe. Linc-3E 17
Skelmanthorpe. W.Yk
-1B 16
Skelmersdale. Lanc-1F 15
Skelmorlie. Stra-1E 23
Skelpick. High-1G 35
Skelton. Clev-2E 21
Skelton. Cumb-1F 19
Skelwith Bridge. Cumb
-2F 19
Skerray. High-1G 35
Skidby. Humb-5F 21
Skigersta. W.Is-1C 34
Skipness. Stra-1D 22
Skipsea. Humb-4G 21
Skipton. N.Yk-4H 19
Slaidburn. Lanc-4G 19
Slaithwaite. W.Yk-1B 16
Slamannan. Cent-1H 23
Sleaford. Linc-1B 12
Sledmere. Humb-4F 21
Sleights. N.Yk-2F 21
Sligachan. High-3D 30
Slough. Berk-2A 6
Smethwick. W.Md-1E 11
Snainton. N.Yk-3F 21
Snaith. Humb-1D 16
Snape. Suff-4G 13
Snettisham. Norf-1D 12

Snodland. Kent-3D 6
Soham. Camb-4D 12
Solihull. W.Md-1E 11
Sollas. W.Is-2B 30
Solva. Dyfd-4B 8
Somercotes. Derb-3C 16
Somersham. Camb-3C 12
Somerton. Som-3B 4
Sonning Common. Oxfd
-5G 11
Sopley. Hamp-5E 5
Sorbie. D&G-1B 18
Sorn. Stra-2G 23
Sortat. High-4B 36
Southam. War-2F 11
Southampton. Hamp-4F 5
South Anston. S.Yk-2D 16
South Benfleet. Essx-2E 7
Southborough. Kent-4D 6
South Cave. Humb-5F 21
South Collingham. Nott
-3E 17
South Elmsall. W.Yk-1C 16
Southend-on-Sea. Essx
-2E 7
Southery. Norf-3D 12
South Ferriby. Humb-1E 17
South Hayling. Hamp-5G 5
South Kelsey. Linc-1F 17
South Kyme. Linc-1B 12
Southminster. Essx-2E 7
South Molton. Devn-1F 3
South Petherton. Som
-4B 4
Southport. Mers-1F 15
South Queensferry. Loth
-5E 29
South Shields. T&W-5H 25
South Skirlaugh. Humb
-5G 21
South Warnborough.
Hamp-3G 5
Southwell. Nott-3D 16
Southwold. Suff-3G 13
South Woodham Ferrers.
Essx-2E 7
South Wootton. Norf
-2D 12
Sowerby Bridge. W.Yk
-1B 16
Spalding. Linc-2B 12
Sparkford. Som-3C 4
Spean Bridge. High-1F 27
Speke. Mers-2F 15
Spennymoor. Dur-1D 20
Spetisbury. Dors-4D 4
Spey Bay. Grmp-3E 33
Spilsby. Linc-3G 17
Spittal. D&G-5F 23
Spittalfield. Tays-3E 29
Spofforth. N.Yk-4D 20
Sproatley. Humb-5G 21
Stadhampton. Oxfd-5G 11
Staffin. High-2D 30
Stafford. Staf-5H 15
Staindrop. Dur-2C 20
Staines. Surr-3B 6
Stainforth. N.Yk-4H 19
Stainforth. S.Yk-1D 16
Staithes. N.Yk-2F 21
Stalbridge. Dors-4C 4
Stalham. Norf-1G 13
Stalybridge. G.Mn-2H 15
Stamford. Linc-2B 12
Stamford Bridge. Humb
-4E 21
Stamfordham. Nmbd
-5G 25
Standish. G.Mn-1G 15
Stanford-le-Hope. Essx
-2D 6
Stanhope. Dur-1H 19
Stanion. Nptn-3A 12
Stanley. Dur-5G 25
Stanley. Tays-3E 29
Stansted Mountfitchet.
Essx-5D 12
Stanton. Suff-4E 13
Stanwick. Nptn-4A 12
Stapleford. Nott-4C 16

Stapleford. Wilt-3E 5
Staplehurst. Kent-4E 7
Starcross. Devn-3G 3
Starkigarth. Shet-4G 37
Staunton. Glos-3D 10
Staunton on Wye. H&W
-3H 9
Staveley. Cumb-3F 19
Staveley. Derb-3C 16
Staverton. Nptn-2G 11
Staxigoe. High-4B 36
Staxton. N.Yk-3G 21
Staylittle. Powy-1F 9
Steeple Bumpstead. Essx
-5D 12
Steeton. W.Yk-5C 20
Stenso. Orkn-1B 36
Stenton. Loth-1E 25
Stevenage. Hert-5B 12
Stevenston. Stra-2F 23
Stewarton. Stra-2F 23
(nr. Kilmarnock)
Stewkley. Buck-5A 12
Steyning. W.Su-5B 6
Stibb Cross. Devn-2E 3
Stichill. Bord-2E 25
Stickney. Linc-3G 17
Stilligarry. W.Is-3B 30
Stillingfleet. N.Yk-5E 21
Stillington. N.Yk-4E 21
Stilton. Camb-3B 12
Stirling. Cent-5D 28
Stockbridge. Hamp-3F 5
Stockport. G.Mn-2H 15
Stocksbridge. S.Yk-2C 16
Stockton-on-Tees. Clev
-2D 20
Stoer. High-2E 35
Stoke Ferry. Norf-3D 12
Stoke Lacy. H&W-3C 10
Stoke Mandeville. Buck
-1A 6
Stokenchurch. Buck-2A 6
Stoke-on-Trent. Staf-4H 15
Stokesley. N.Yk-2E 21
Stone. Buck-1A 6
Stone. Glos-5C 10
Stone. Staf-4H 15
Stonehaven. Grmp-1H 29
Stonehouse. Wilt-5E 11
Stoneybridge. W.Is-3A 30
Stoneykirk. D&G-1A 18
Stoney Stanton. Leic-1F 11
Stonybreck. Shet-3D 36
Stornoway. W.Is-2B 34
Storrington. W.Su-5B 6
Stotfold. Beds-5B 12
Stourbridge. W.Md-1D 10
Stourport-on-Severn.
H&W-2D 10
Stow. Bord-2D 24
Stow. Linc-2E 17
Stowmarket. Suff-4F 13
Stow-on-the-Wold. Glos
-3E 11
Stowupland. Suff-4F 13
Strachan. Grmp-1G 29
Strachur. Stra-5D 16
Stradbroke. Suff-4F 13
Straiton. Stra-3F 23
Stranraer. D&G-5E 23
Stratford. G.Ln-2C 6
Stratford-upon-Avon. War
-2E 11
Strathaven. Stra-2G 23
Strathblane. Cent-5C 28
Strathcarron. High-3F 31
Strathdon. Grmp-5E 33
Strath Kanaird. High-3E 35
Strathpeffer. High-3A 32
Strathy. High-1H 35
(nr. Melvich)
Strathyre. Cent-4C 28
Stratton. Corn-2D 2
Stratton St Margaret. Wilt
-5E 11
Street. Som-3B 4
Stretham. Camb-4D 12
Stretton-on-Dunsmore.
War-2F 11
Strichen. Grmp-3G 33
Stromeferry. High-3F 31

Stromemore. High-3F 31
Stromness. Orkn-2A 36
Stronachlachar. Cent
-4B 28
Strontian. High-2E 27
Strood. Kent-3D 6
Stroud. Glos-4D 10
Struy. High-4A 32
Stuartfield. Grmp-4G 33
Studland. Dors-5E 5
Studley. War-2E 11
Sturry. Kent-3F 7
Sturton by Stow. Linc
-2E 17
Sudbury. Derb-4B 16
Sudbury. Suff-5E 13
Sulby. IOM-3B 18
Summer Bridge. N.Yk
-4C 20
Sunderland. T&W-5H 25
Sunninghill. Berk-3A 6
Sutterton. Linc-1C 12
Sutton. Camb-3C 12
Sutton. G.Ln-3C 6
Sutton Bridge. Linc-2C 12
Sutton Coldfield. W.Md
-1E 11
Sutton in Ashfield. Nott
-3C 16
Sutton-in-Craven. N.Yk
-5C 20
Sutton on Sea. Linc-2H 17
Sutton-on-the-Forest. N.Yk
-4E 21
Sutton on Trent. Nott
-3E 17
Sutton St James. Linc
-2C 12
Sutton Scotney. Hamp
-3F 5
Sutton Valence. Kent-4E 7
Swadlincote. Derb-5C 16
Swaffham. Norf-2E 13
Swainby. N.Yk-2D 20
Swanage. Dors-5E 5
Swanley. Kent-3D 6
Swansea. W.Gl-5E 9
Swanton Morley. Norf
-2F 13
Swindon. Wilt-5E 11
Swinefleet. Humb-1E 17
Swineshead. Linc-1B 12
Swinton. Bord-2F 25
Swinton. S.Yk-2C 16
Symbister. Shet-3H 37
Syre. High-2G 35
Syston. Leic-5D 16

Tadcaster. N.Yk-5D 20
Tain. High-2C 32
(nr. Invergordon)
Talgarth. Powy-3G 9
Talisker. High-3D 30
Talladale. High-2F 31
Talley. Dyfd-3E 9
Talmine. High-1G 35
Talsarnau. Gwyn-4C 14
Talybont. Dyfd-1E 9
Tal-y-bont. Gwyn-3B 14
Talysarn. Gwyn-3B 14
Tamworth. Staf-5B 16
Tannadice. Tays-2F 29
Tarbert. High-1D 22
(on Knapdale)
Tarbert. W.Is-3A 34
Tarbet. Stra-4B 28
Tarbolton. Stra-2F 23
Tarland. Grmp-5E 33
Tarleton. Lanc-1F 15
Tarporley. Ches-3G 15
Tarskavaig. High-4E 31
Tarves. Grmp-4G 33
Tarvin. Ches-3F 15
Tattenhall. Ches-3F 15
Tattershall. Linc-3F 17
Taunton. Som-3A 4
Tavistock. Devn-4E 3
Tayinloan. Stra-2C 22
Taynuilt. Stra-4F 26
Tayport. Fife-3F 29
Tayvallich. Stra-5D 26

Tealby. Linc-2F 17
Teangue. High-4E 31
Teesport. Clev-2E 21
Teignmouth. Devn-4G 3
Telford. Shrp-5G 15
Templand. D&G-4C 24
Temple Ewell. Kent-4G 7
Templeton. Dyfd-4C 8
Tenbury Wells. H&W
-2C 10
Tenby. Dyfd-4C 8
Tenterden. Kent-4E 7
Terrington St Clement.
Norf-2D 12
Terrington St John. Norf
-2D 12
Tetbury. Glos-5D 10
Tetford. Linc-3G 17
Tetney. Linc-1G 17
Teviothead. Bord-3D 24
Tewkesbury. Glos-3D 10
Thame. Oxfd-4G 11
Thamesport. Kent-3E 7
Thatcham. Berk-2G 5
Thaxted. Essx-5D 12
Theale. Berk-2G 5
Thetford. Norf-3E 13
Thirsk. N.Yk-3D 20
Thornaby-on-Tees. Clev
-2D 20
Thornbury. Avon-5C 10
Thorne. S.Yk-1D 16
Thorney. Cambs-2C 12
Thorngumbald. Humb
-5G 21
Thornhill. Cent-4C 28
Thornhill. D&G-4H 23
Thornton. Fife-5F 29
Thornton. Lanc-5F 19
Thornton-le-Dale. N.Yk
-3F 21
Thorpe-le-Soken. Essx
-1F 7
Thrapston. Nptn-3A 12
Threlkeld. Cumb-1F 19
Threshfield. N.Yk-4H 19
Thropton. Nmbd-3G 25
Thrumster. High-5B 36
Thruxton. Hamp-3F 5
Thurcroft. S.Yk-2C 16
Thurlestone. Devn-5F 3
Thurnby. Leic-5D 16
Thurso. High-4A 36
Tibshelf. Derb-3C 16
Ticehurst. E.Su-4D 6
Tickhill. S.Yk-2D 16
Tideswell. Derb-3B 16
Tigharry. W.Is-2A 30
Tighnabruaich. Stra-1D 22
Tilbury. Essx-2D 6
Tillicoultry. Cent-5D 28
Tillyfourie. Grmp-5F 33
Tilton on the Hill. Leic
-5D 16
Timberscombe. Som-1G 3
Timsgarry. W.Is-2A 34
Tingwall. Orkn-2B 36
Tintagel. Corn-3D 2
Tinwald. D&G-4C 24
Tipton. W.Md-1D 10
Tiptree. Essx-1E 7
Tiverton. Devn-2G 3
Toab. Shet-5G 37
Tobermory. Stra-2C 26
Toddington. Beds-5B 12
Todmorden. W.Yk-1H 15
Toft. Shet-2G 37
Tollesbury. Essx-1E 7
Tolsta Chaolais. W.Is
-2A 34
Tomatin. High-4C 32
Tomdoun. High-4G 31
Tomich. High-4A 32
(nr. Cannich)
Tomintoul. Grmp-5D 32
Tomnavoulin. Grmp-4D 32
Tonbridge. Kent-4D 6
Tondu. M.Gl-5F 9
Tongland. D&G-5G 23
Tongue. High-1G 35
Tonypandy. M.Gl-5F 9

Topcliffe. N.Yk-3D 20
Topsham. Devn-3G 3
Torcross. Devn-5G 3
Tore. High-3B 32
Torphichen. Loth-1H 23
Torphins. Grmp-5F 33
Torpoint. Corn-4E 3
Torquay. Devn-4G 3
Torridon. High-2F 31
Torrin. High-4E 31
Torthorwald. D&G-4C 24
Toscaig. High-3E 31
Totnes. Devn-4G 3
Tottenham. G.Ln-2C 6
Totton. Hamp-4F 5
Towcester. Nptn-3G 11
Towie. Grmp-5E 33
Tow Law. Dur-1C 20
Town Yetholm. Bord-2F 25
Trafford Park. G.Mn-2H 15
Tranent. Loth-1D 24
Trawden. Lanc-5H 19
Trawsfynydd. Gwyn-4C 14
Trearddur. Gwyn-2B 14
Trecastle. Powy-3F 9
Tredegar. Gwnt-4G 9
Trefeglwys. Powy-1F 9
Trefnant. Clwd-3E 15
Trefor. Gwyn-4B 14
Tregaron. Dyfd-2E 9
Tregynon. Powy-1G 9
Treherbert. M.Gl-5F 9
Tremadog. Gwyn-4C 14
Tremeirchion. Clwd-3E 15
Treorchy. M.Gl-5F 9
Tresta. Shet-3G 37
 (on Mainland)
Trevine. Dyfd-3B 8
Trimdon. Dur-1D 20
Trimley St Mary. Suff
 -5G 13
Tring. Hert-1A 6
Trochry. Tays-3D 28
Troon. Stra-2F 23
Troutbeck. Cumb-2F 19
Trowbridge. Wilt-2D 4
Truro. Corn-5C 2
Tudweiliog. Gwyn-4A 14
Tullynessle. Grmp-5F 33
Tumble. Dyfd-4E 9
Tummel Bridge. Tays
 -2D 28
Tunga. W.Is-2B 34
Tunstall. Staf-3H 15
Tunstall. Suff-4G 13
Turnberry. Stra-3E 23
Turriff. Grmp-3F 33
Tutbury. Staf-4B 16
Tuxford. Nott-3D 17
Tweedmouth. Nmbd-1F 25
Twickenham. G.Ln-3B 6
Two Bridges. Devn-4F 3
Twycross. Leic-5C 16
Twyford. Berk-2A 6
Twyford. Hamp-4F 5
Twynholm. D&G-5G 23
Tydd St Giles. Camb-2C 12
Tyldesley. G.Mn-1G 15
Tyndrum. Cent-3B 28
Tynemouth. T&W-5H 25
Tynron. D&G-4H 23
Tywyn. Gwyn-5C 14

Uckfield. E.Su-5C 6
Uffculme. Devn-4A 4
Uffington. Linc-2B 12

Uig. High-2D 30
 (nr. Glen Uig)
Ulbster. High-5B 36
Ulceby. Humb-1F 17
Ulgham. Nmbd-4G 25
Ullapool. High-1G 31
Ullesthorpe. Leic-1F 11
Ulsta. Shet-2G 37
Ulverston. Cumb-3F 19
Upavon. Wilt-2E 5
Uphall. Loth-1C 24
Upminster. G.Ln-2D 6
Upper Chapel. Powy-3G 9
Upper Killay. W.Gl-5E 9
Upper Ollach. High-3E 31
Upper Tean. Staf-4B 16
Uppingham. Leic-3A 12
Upwell. Camb-2C 12
Urchfont. Wilt-2E 5
Urmston. G.Mn-2G 15
Usk. Gwnt-4H 9
Uttoxeter. Staf-4B 16
Uxbridge. G.Ln-2B 6

Valtos. W.Is-2A 34
Veensgarth. Shet-4G 37
Ventnor. IOW-5G 5
Verwood. Dors-4E 5
Vickerstown. Cumb-4E 19
Vidlin. Shet-3G 37
Virginia Water. Surr-3A 6
Voe. Shet-3G 37
 (nr. Tresta)

Waddesdon. Buck-4G 11
Waddington. Lanc-5G 19
Waddington. Linc-3E 17
Wadebridge. Corn-4C 2
Wadhurst. E.Su-4D 6
Wainfleet All Saints. Linc
 -3G 17
Wakefield. W.Yk-1C 16
Walberswick. Suff-4G 13
Wales. S.Yk-2C 16
Walkden. G.Mn-1G 15
Wallasey. Mers-2F 15
Wallingford. Oxfd-5G 11
Walls. Shet-4F 37
Wallsend. T&W-5H 25
Walsall. W.Md-1E 11
Waltham. Humb-1F 17
Waltham Abbey. Essx-1C 6
Waltham on the Wolds.
 Leic-2A 12
Walton. Powy-2H 9
Walton-on-Thames. Surr
 -3B 6
Walton-on-the-Naze. Essx
 -1F 7
Wandsworth. G.Ln-3C 6
Wangford. Suff-3G 13
Wanlockhead. D&G-3H 23
Wansford. Camb-3B 12
Wanstrow. Som-3C 4
Wantage. Oxfd-5F 11
Warboys. Camb-3B 12
Warcop. Cumb-2H 19
Ware. Hert-1C 6
Wareham. Dors-5D 4
Waren Mill. Nmbd-2G 25
Wargrave. Berk-2A 6
Wark. Nmbd-4F 25
Warkworth. Nmbd-3H 25
Warlingham. Surr-3C 6
Warmington. Nptn-3B 12
Warminster. Wilt-3D 4

Warrington. Ches-2G 15
Warsop. Nott-3D 16
Warton. Lanc-5F 19
Warwick. War-2F 11
Warwick Bridge. Cumb
 -5D 24
Wasbister. Orkn-1B 36
Washford. Som-3A 4
Washingborough. Linc
 -3F 17
Washington. T&W-5H 25
Washington. W.Su-5B 6
Watchet. Som-3A 4
Watchfield. Oxfd-5E 11
Waterbeach. Camb-4C 12
Waterbeck. D&G-4D 24
Waterlooville. Hamp-4G 5
Waterside. Stra-3F 23
 (nr. Ayr)
Watford. Hert-2B 6
Wath upon Dearne. S.Yk
 -1C 16
Watlington. Oxfd-5G 11
Watten. High-4A 36
Watton. Norf-2E 13
Watton at Stone. Hert
 -1C 6
Waverton. Ches-4F 15
Weaverham. Ches-3G 15
Wedmore. Som-3B 4
Wednesbury. W.Md-1D 10
Wednesfield. W.Md-5H 15
Weedon Bec. Nptn-2G 11
Week St Mary. Corn-3D 2
Weeley. Essx-1F 7
Weem. Tays-3D 28
Weeting. Norf-3E 13
Weldon. Nptn-3A 12
Welford. Nptn-1G 11
Welland. H&W-3D 10
Wellesbourne. War-2F 11
Wellingborough. Nptn
 -4A 12
Wellingore. Linc-3E 17
Wellington. Shrp-5G 15
Wellington. Som-4A 4
Wells. Som-3C 4
Wells-next-the-Sea. Norf
 -1E 13
Welshampton. Shrp-4F 15
Welshpool. Powy-5E 15
Welton. Humb-5F 21
Welton. Linc-2F 17
Welwyn. Hert-1B 6
Welwyn Garden City. Hert
 -1B 6
Wem. Shrp-4G 15
Wendover. Buck-1A 6
West Auckland. Dur-1C 20
West Ayton. N.Yk-3F 21
West Bergholt. Essx
 -5E 13
West Bridgford. Nott
 -4D 16
West Bromwich. W.Md
 -1E 11
West Burrafirth. Shet
 -3G 37
Westbury. Shrp-5F 15
Westbury. Wilt-2D 4
Westbury-sub-Mendip.
 Som-3B 4
West Calder. Loth-1C 24
Westerdale. High-4A 36
Westerham. Kent-3C 6
Wester Pencaitland. Loth
 -1D 24

Westfield. High-4A 36
Westgate on Sea. Kent
 -3G 7
West Gerinish. W.Is
 -3B 30
West Haddon. Nptn-2G 11
West Harptree. Avon-2C 4
Westhill. Grmp-5G 33
Westhoughton. G.Mn
 -1G 15
West Kilbride. Stra-2E 23
West Kingsdown. Kent
 -3D 6
West Kirby. Mers-2E 15
West Linton. Bord-1C 24
West Lulworth. Dors-5D 4
West Meon. Hamp-4G 5
West Mersea. Essx-1F 7
Westminster. G.Ln-2C 6
West Moors. Dors-4E 5
Westnewton. Cumb-1E 19
Weston. Staf-4H 15
Weston-super-Mare. Avon
 -2B 4
Westonzoyland. Som-3B 4
West Pennard. Som-3C 4
Westruther. Bord-1E 25
West Tarbert. Stra-1D 22
Westward Ho!. Devn-1E 3
West Winch. Norf-2D 12
West Woodburn. Nmbd
 -4F 25
Westwoodside. Humb
 -2D 16
Wetheral. Cumb-5D 24
Wetherby. W.Yk-5D 20
Wetwang. Humb-4F 21
Weybourne. Norf-1F 13
Weybridge. Surr-3B 6
Weymouth. Dors-5C 4
Whaley Bridge. Derb
 -2B 16
Whalley. Lanc-5G 19
Whalton. Nmbd-4G 25
Whaplode. Linc-2C 12
Whauphill. D&G-1B 18
Wheathampstead. Hert
 -1B 6
Wheatley. Oxfd-4G 11
Wheatley Hill. Dur-1D 20
Wheaton Aston. Staf
 -5H 15
Wheddon Cross. Som
 -1G 3
Whickham. T&W-5G 25
Whitburn. Loth-1H 23
Whitburn. T&W-5H 25
Whitby. N.Yk-2F 21
Whitchurch. Buck-1A 6
Whitchurch. Hamp-3F 5
Whitchurch. H&W-4C 10
Whitchurch. Shrp-4G 15
Whitefield. G.Mn-1H 15
Whitehall. Orkn-1C 36
Whitehaven. Cumb-2D 18
Whitehills. Grmp-3F 33
Whitehouse. Stra-1D 22
Whitekirk. Loth-5G 29
Whiteparish. Wilt-4F 5
Whithorn. D&G-1B 18
Whiting Bay. Stra-2E 23
Whitland. Dyfd-4C 8
Whitley Bay. T&W-5H 25
Whitminster. Bord-1F 25
Whitstable. Kent-3F 7
Whittingham. Nmbd
 -3G 25
Whittington. Shrp-4F 15

Whittle-le-Woods. Lanc
 -1G 15
Whittlesey. Camb-3C 12
Whitton. Powy-2H 9
Whitwell. Derb-2D 16
Whitwick. Leic-5C 16
Whitworth. Lanc-1H 15
Wick. Avon-2C 4
Wick. High-5B 36
Wick. M.Gl-5F 9
Wicken. Camb-4D 12
Wickford. Essx-2D 6
Wickham Market. Suff
 -4G 13
Widdrington. Nmbd
 -4H 25
Widecombe in the Moor.
 Devn-4F 3
Widnes. Ches-2F 15
Wigan. G.Mn-1G 15
Wigmore. H&W-2H 9
Wigston. Leic-1G 11
Wigton. Cumb-1F 19
Wigtown. D&G-5F 23
Wilberfoss. Humb-4E 21
Wilkhaven. High-2C 32
Willaston. Ches-2F 15
Willenhall. W.Md-1D 10
Willingham. Camb-4C 12
Willington. Derb-4C 16
Willington. Dur-1C 20
Williton. Som-3A 4
Wilmslow. Ches-2H 15
Wilpshire. Lanc-5G 19
Wilstead. Beds-5B 12
Wilton. Wilt-3E 5
Wimbledon. G.Ln-3C 6
Wimblington. Camb-3C 12
Wimborne Minster. Dors
 -4E 5
Wincanton. Som-3C 4
Winchcombe. Glos-3E 11
Winchelsea. E.Su-5E 7
Winchester. Hamp-3F 5
Windermere. Cumb-2F 19
Windsor. Berk-2A 6
Windygates. Fife-4F 29
Wing. Buck-1A 6
Wingate. Dur-1D 20
Wingerworth. Derb-3C 16
Wingham. Kent-3F 7
Winkleigh. Devn-2F 3
Winscombe. Avon-2B 4
Winsford. Ches-3G 15
Winsford. Som-1G 3
Winsham. Som-4B 4
Winslow. Buck-5A 12
Winston. Dur-2C 20
Winterbourne Abbas. Dors
 -5C 4
Winteringham. Humb
 -1E 17
Winterton. Humb-1E 17
Winterton-on-Sea. Norf
 -2G 13
Wirksworth. Derb-3C 16
Wisbech. Camb-2C 12
Wishaw. Stra-1H 23
Wistanstow. Shrp-1H 9
Wistow. N.Yk-5E 21
Witchford. Camb-3D 12
Witham. Essx-1E 7
Witheridge. Devn-2G 3
Withernsea. Humb-5H 21
Withypool. Som-1G 3
Witney. Oxfd-4F 11
Wittering. Camb-2B 12

Wiveliscombe. Som-3A 4
Wivenhoe. Essx-1F 7
Woburn. Beds-5A 12
Woburn Sands. Buck
 -5A 12
Woking. Surr-3B 6
Wokingham. Berk-3A 6
Wolferton. Norf-1D 12
Wollaston. Nptn-4A 12
Wolsingham. Dur-1C 20
Wolston. War-1F 11
Wolverhampton. W.Md
 -1D 10
Wolvey. War-1F 11
Wombwell. S.Yk-1C 16
Wonersh. Surr-4B 6
Woodbridge. Suff-5G 13
Woodford. G.Ln-2C 6
Woodhall Spa. Linc-3F 17
Woodingdean. E.Su-5C 6
Woodland. Dur-1C 20
Woodstock. Oxfd-4F 11
Wool. Dors-5D 4
Woolacombe. Devn-1E 3
Wooler. Nmbd-2F 25
Woolfardisworthy.
 -2E 3
Woolwich. G.Ln-2C 6
Woore. Shrp-4G 15
Wootton. Nptn-4A 12
Wootton Bassett. Wilt
 -5E 11
Worcester. H&W-2D 10
Workington. Cumb-1D 18
Worksop. Nott-2D 16
Worsbrough. S.Yk-1C 16
Worthen. Shrp-5F 15
Worthing. W.Su-5B 6
Wotton-under-Edge. Glos
 -5D 10
Wragby. Linc-2F 17
Wrangle. Linc-3G 17
Wrea Green. Lanc-5F 19
Wrentham. Suff-3G 13
Wrexham. Clwd-3F 15
Writtle. Essx-1D 6
Wroughton. Wilt-5E 11
Wroxham. Norf-2G 13
Wyberton. Linc-1C 12
Wybunbury. Ches-4G 15
Wychbold. H&W-2D 10
Wych Cross. E.Su-4C 6
Wye. Kent-4F 7
Wymeswold. Leic-5D 16
Wymondham. Norf-2F 13

Yalding. Kent-3D 6
Yarcombe. Devn-4A 4
Yarm. Clev-2D 20
Yarmouth. IOW-5F 5
Yate. Avon-5C 10
Yatton. Avon-2B 4
Yaxley. Camb-3B 12
Yeadon. W.Yk-5C 20
Yealmpton. Devn-4F 3
Yeovil. Som-4C 4
Y Ffor. Gwyn-4B 14
Ynysybwl. M.Gl-5G 9
York. N.Yk-4E 21
Youlgreave. Derb-3B 16
Yoxall. Staf-5B 16
Yoxford. Suff-4G 13
Ysbyty Ifan. Gwyn-4H 15
Ystalyfera. W.Gl-4F 9
Ystradgynlais. Powy-4F 9
Ythanbank. Grmp-4G 33
Ythanwells. Grmp-4F 33

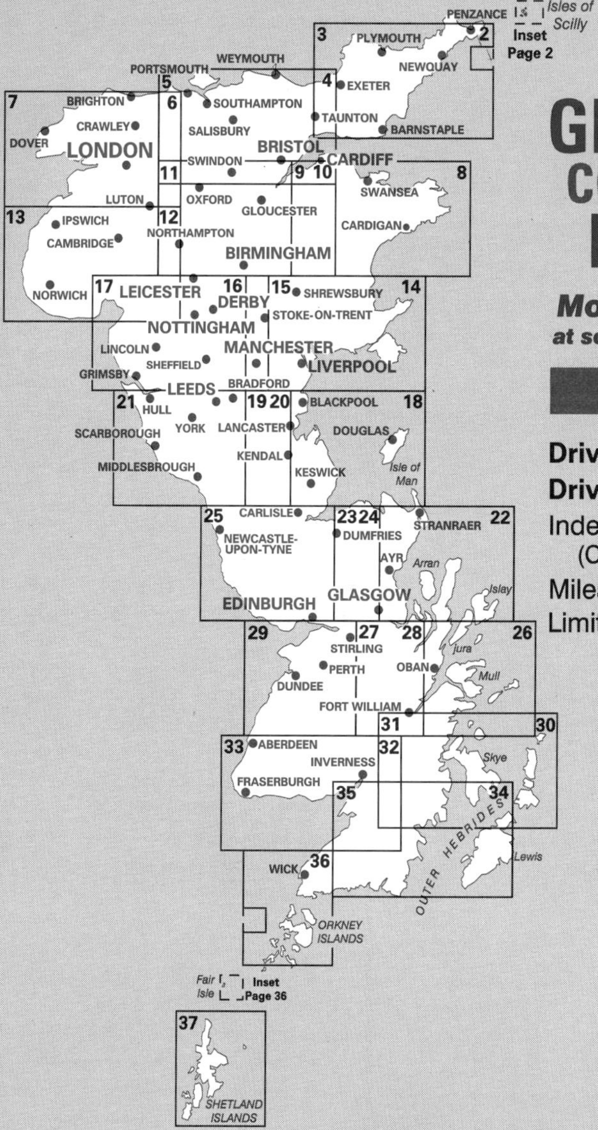

Isles of Scilly

PENZANCE

Inset Page 2

3 PLYMOUTH
WEYMOUTH
NEWQUAY
2

PORTSMOUTH
5
4 EXETER
BRIGHTON
6 SOUTHAMPTON
TAUNTON
7
CRAWLEY
SALISBURY
BARNSTAPLE
DOVER
LONDON
SWINDON
BRISTOL
CARDIFF
11
OXFORD
9 10
8
LUTON
GLOUCESTER
SWANSEA
12
IPSWICH
NORTHAMPTON
13
CAMBRIDGE
BIRMINGHAM
CARDIGAN

NORWICH
17 LEICESTER
16 15 SHREWSBURY
14
DERBY
NOTTINGHAM
STOKE-ON-TRENT
LINCOLN
MANCHESTER
SHEFFIELD
LIVERPOOL
GRIMSBY
LEEDS
BRADFORD
21 HULL
19 20 BLACKPOOL
18
SCARBOROUGH
YORK
LANCASTER
DOUGLAS
MIDDLESBROUGH
KENDAL
KESWICK
Isle of Man

25 CARLISLE
23 24
22
NEWCASTLE-UPON-TYNE
DUMFRIES
STRANRAER
AYR
Arran
EDINBURGH
GLASGOW
Islay
29
27 28
26
STIRLING
Jura
PERTH
OBAN
Mull
DUNDEE
FORT WILLIAM
Skye
31
30
33 ABERDEEN
32
INVERNESS
FRASERBURGH
35
34
Lewis
WICK
36
OUTER HEBRIDES

ORKNEY ISLANDS

Fair Isle
Inset Page 36

37

SHETLAND ISLANDS

GREAT BRITAIN
COMING and GOING
ROAD ATLAS

Motorways and Main Roads
at scale 1:730,000 11.5 miles to 1 inch

CONTENTS

Geographers' A-Z Map Company Ltd.

Head Office:
Fairfield Road, Borough Green, Sevenoaks,
Kent. TN15 8PP Tel. 0732 781000

Showrooms:
44 Gray's Inn Road, London, WC1X 8LR
Tel. 071-242 9246

An A to Z Publication   Edition 1   1994

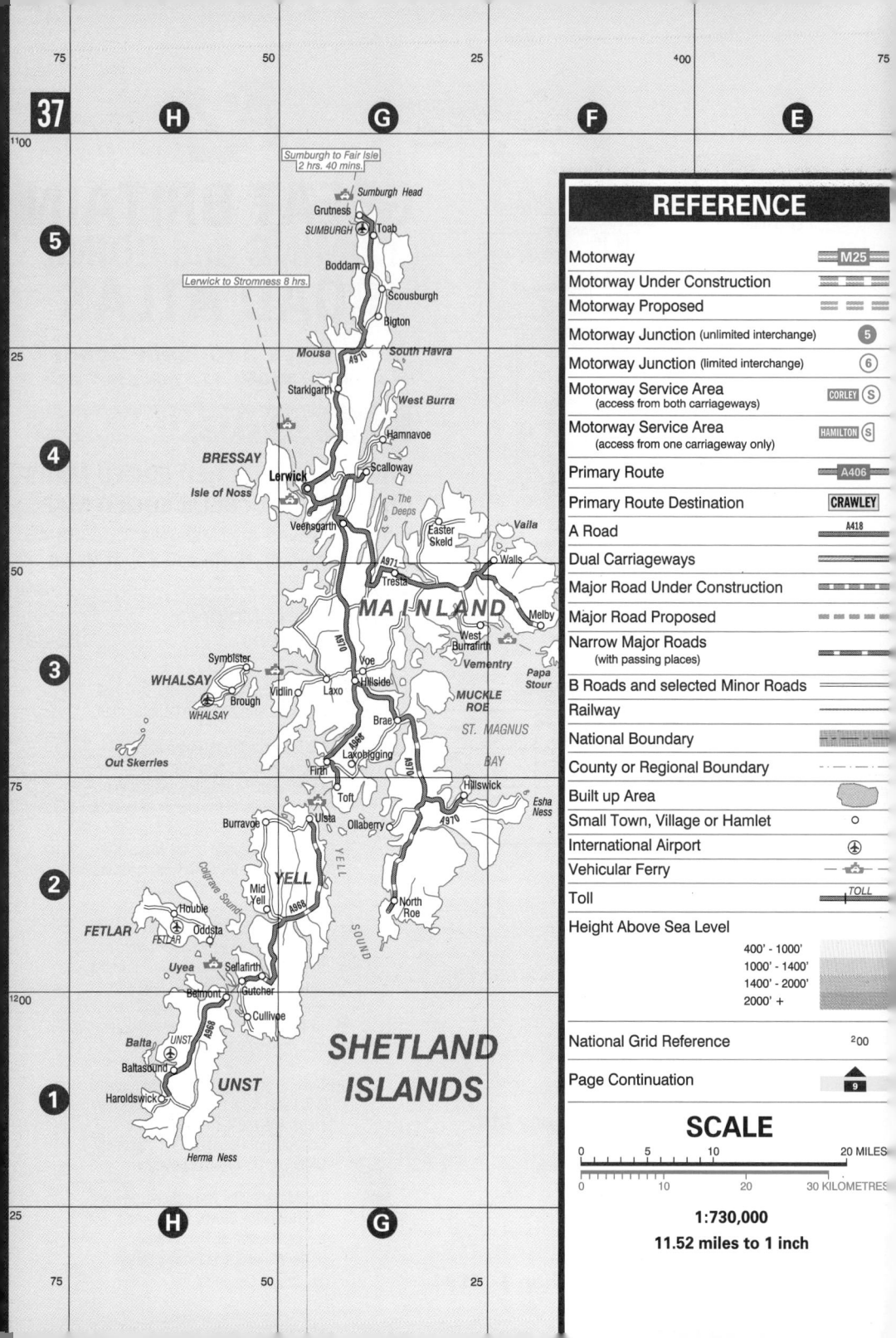

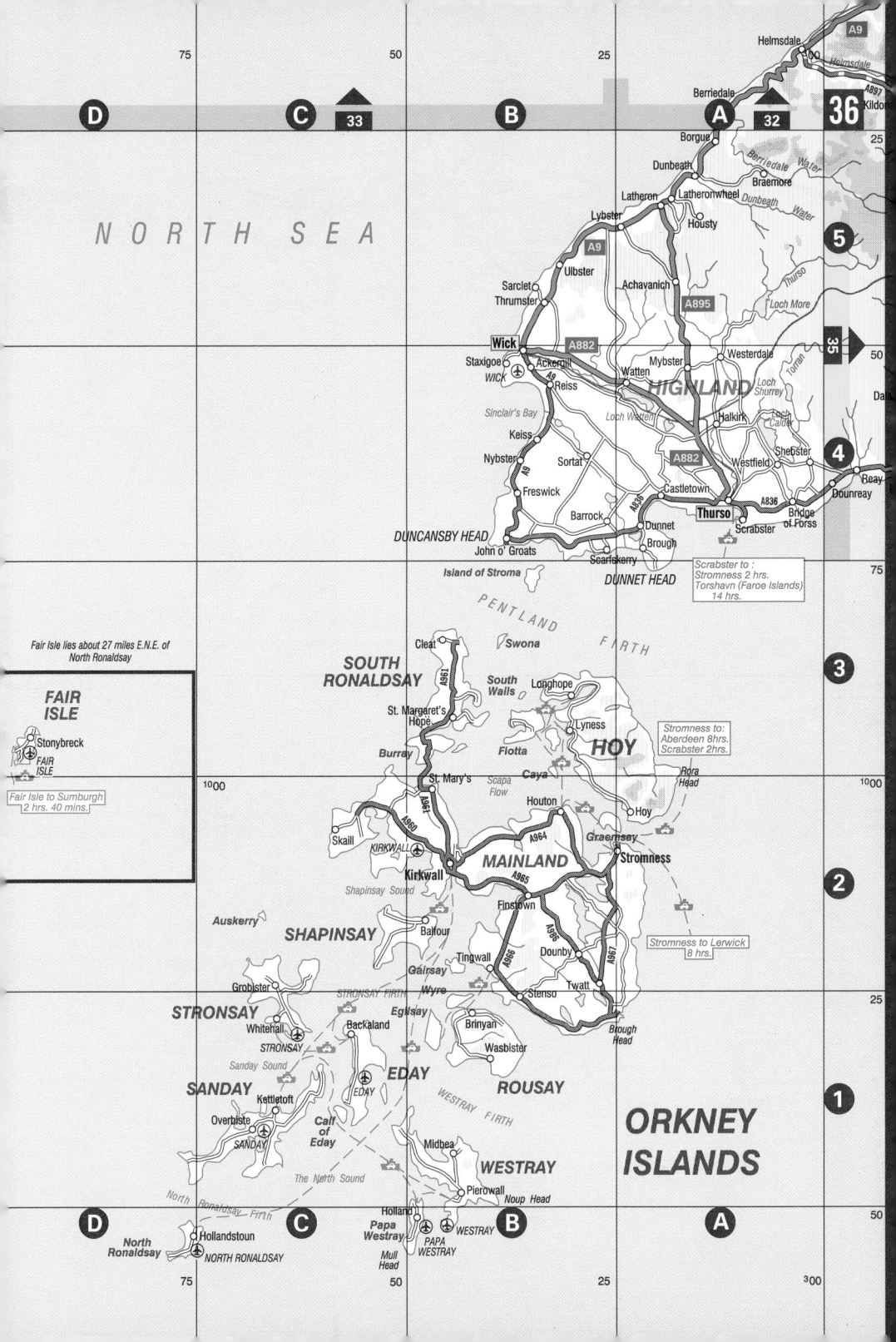

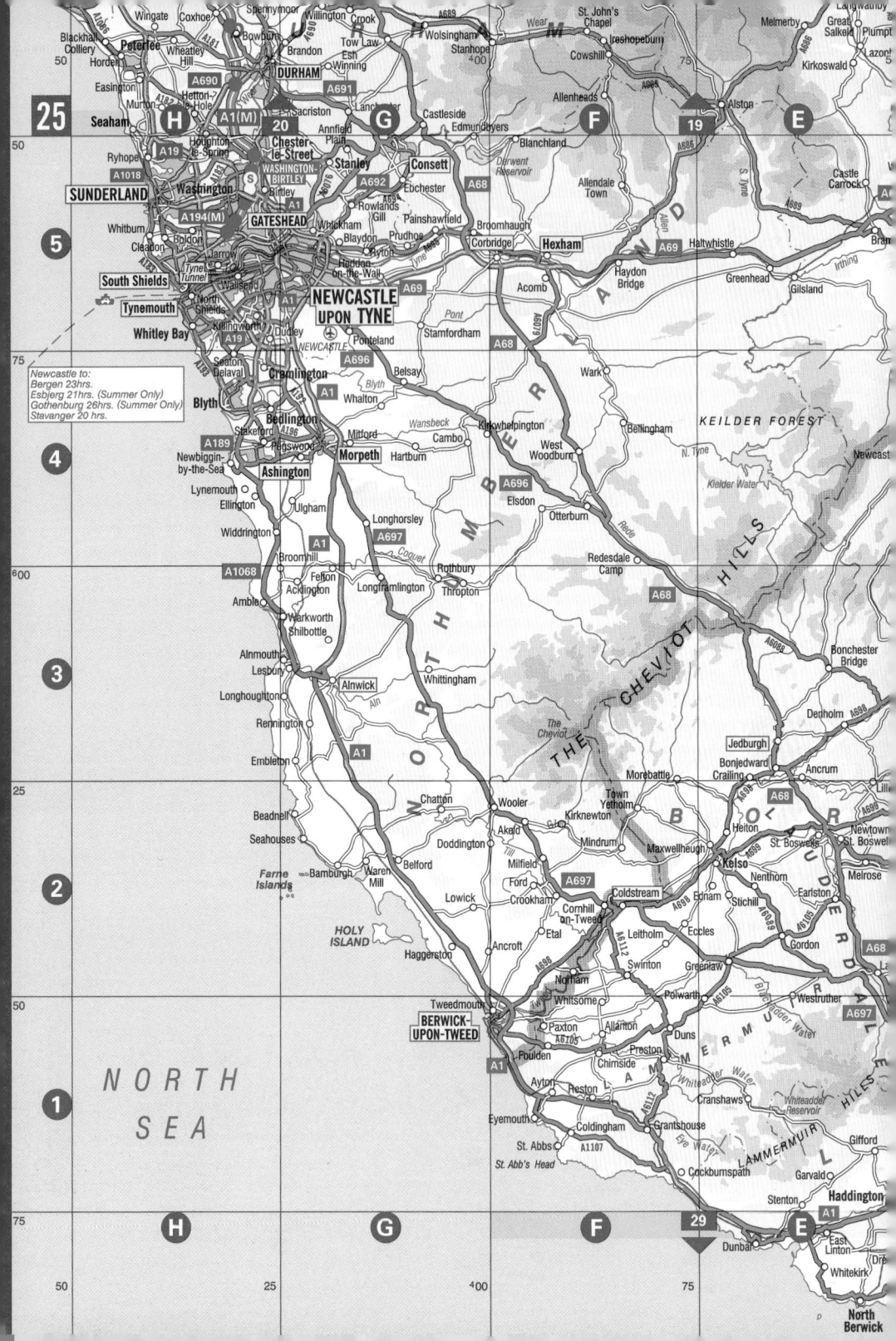

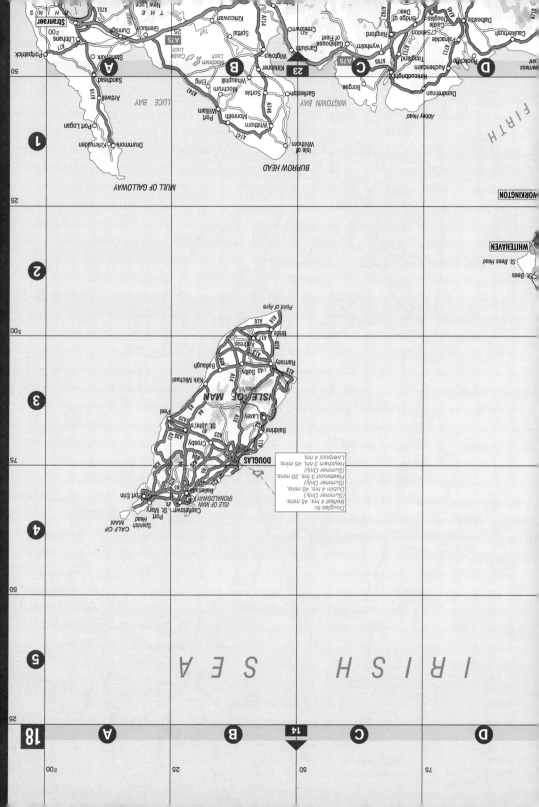

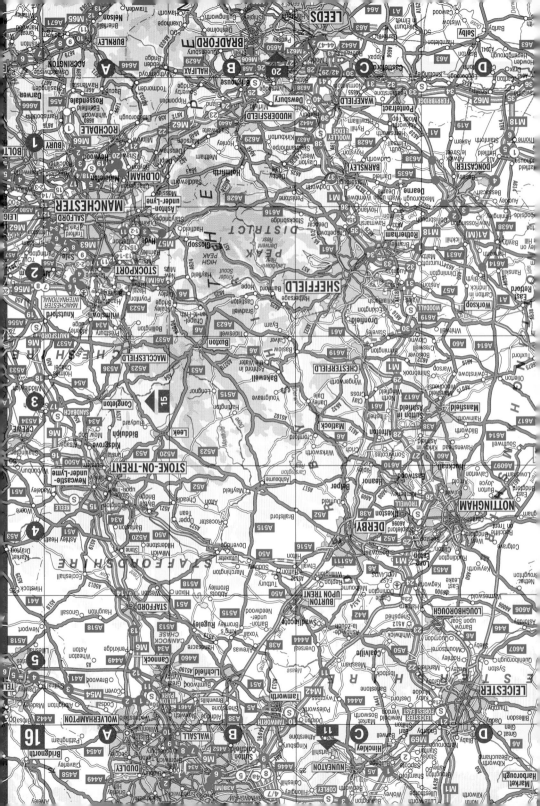

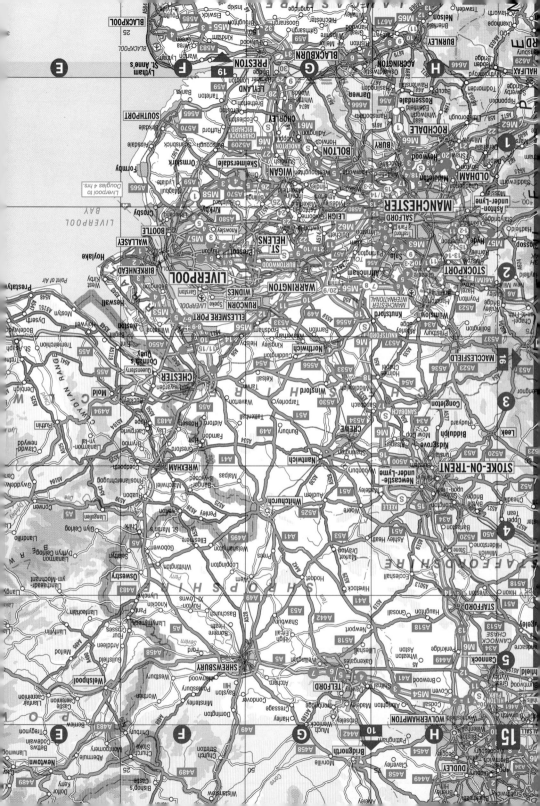

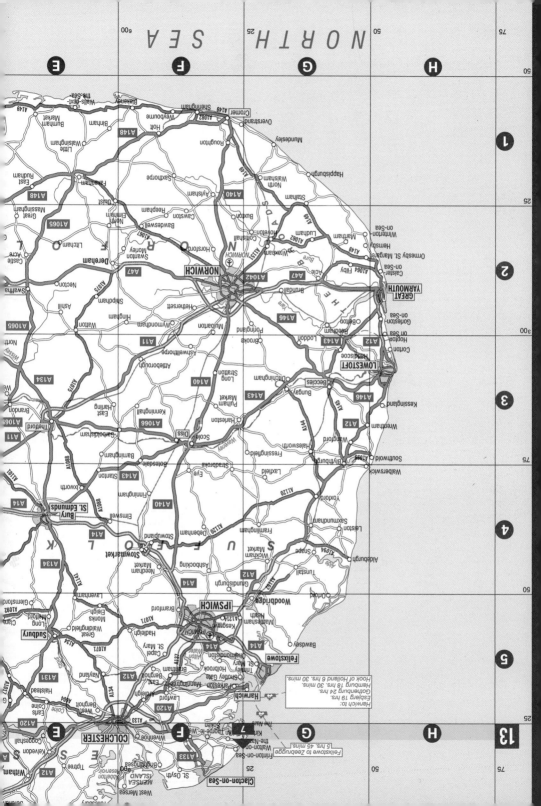

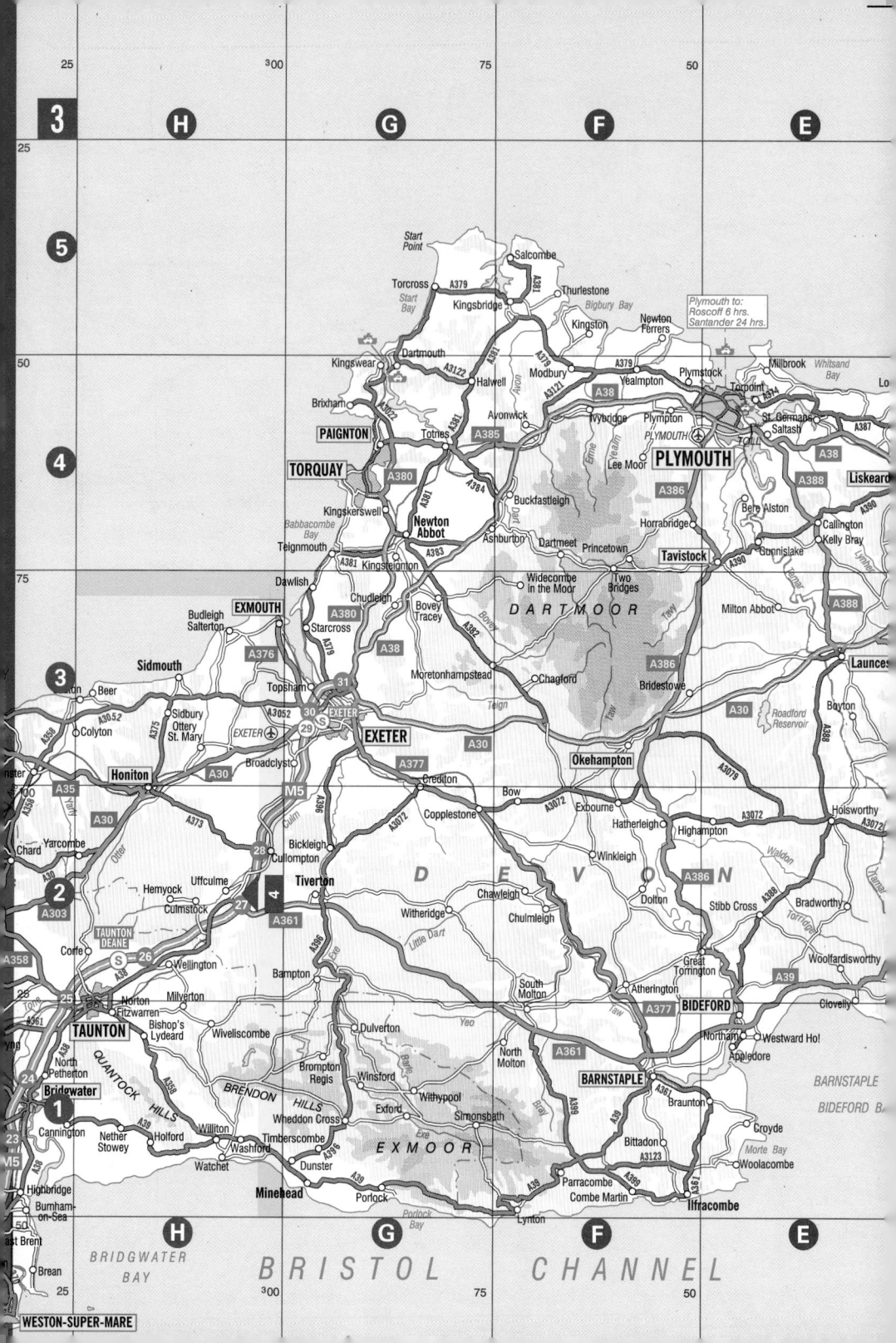

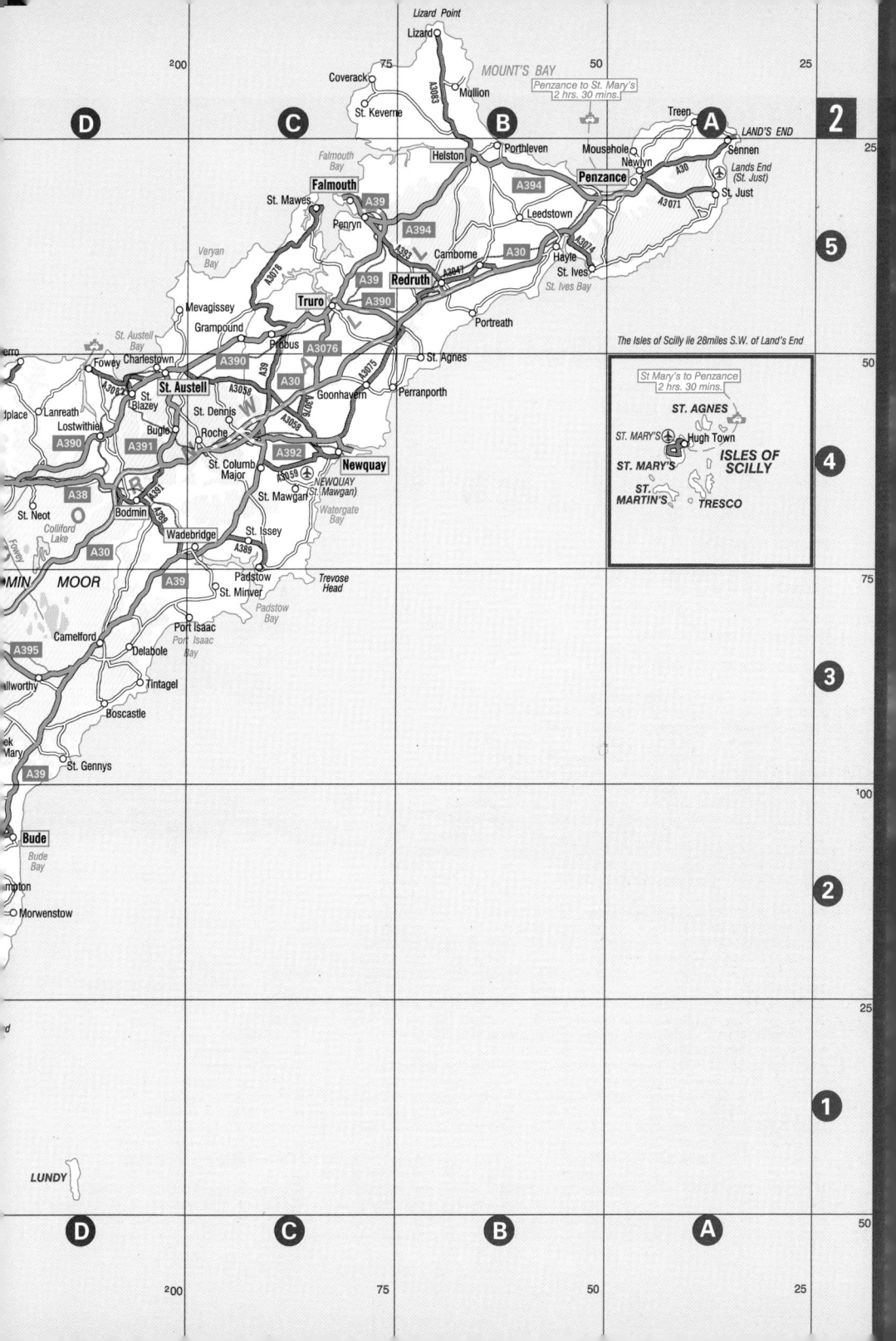

Mileage Chart

The distances for the mileage chart have been compiled by using a combination of Primary Routes and Motorways between any two towns shown.

To find the distance between any two towns shown. Follow the horizontal line of one town and the vertical line of the other, at the intersection read off the mileage.

ie : Horizontal - LONDON

Vertical - Liverpool

Intersection 205 miles

PRIMARY ROUTES, shown in green throughout this Atlas, are a national network of recommended through routes which complement the motorway system. Selected places of major traffic importance are known as Primary Route Destinations and, on road signs, have a green background.

```
ABERDEEN
439  ABERYSTWYTH
175 314  AYR
403 116 279  BIRMINGHAM
326 169 193 124  BRADFORD
588 257 463 169 263  BRIGHTON
503 125 369  88 215 139  BRISTOL
451 213 366 102 156 117 167  CAMBRIDGE
513 109 389 106 233 180  43 201  CARDIFF
218 224  91 193 107 370 275 256 278  CARLISLE
437 134 303  19 124 157 102  84 129 215  COVENTRY
404 137 274  39  88 188 134  99 159 184  43  DERBY
340 192 239  95  39 232 184 117 210 147  94  57  DONCASTER
570 315 484 169 284  77 194 118 233 393 180 208 244  DOVER
125 340  73 284 198 466 374 326 367  91 303 266 212 441  EDINBURGH
569 199 442 161 282 166  75 232 118 351 166 213 257 242 439  EXETER
166 422 136 391 305 568 478 456 493 198 413 382 345 591 132 549  FORT WILLIAM
145 322  35 291 205 468 378 355 393  98  313 282 245 491  46 449 102  GLASGOW
450 108 326  52 171 152  35 132  56 240  60  86 149 189 331 107 438 338  GLOUCESTER
515 281 434 170 224 130 203  64 234 326 152 167 185 129 394 262 524 419 179  HARWICH
443 107 316 151 158 322 207 252 209 225 167 156 169 358 316 279 423 323 180 331  HOLYHEAD
357 235 250 134  68 259 216 134 239 157 122 100  46 254 230 290 357 255 195 204 218  HULL
104 480 202 449 353 620 536 481 551 246 458 421 367 595 154 607  63 167 496 549 481 384  INVERNESS
505 267 420 156 210 125 206  55 240 311 138 155 171 127 381 264 549 409 177  21 307 189 536  IPSWICH
262 182 135 151  62 324 235 215 232  44 170 136  99 344 135 307 242 142 200 279 180 127 290 268  KENDAL
316 171 202 120   9 256 209 144 226 111 117  75  30 275 190 279 311 208 167 208 162  60 345 197  69  LEEDS
407 155 305  43  99 163 118  70 140 214  24  28  73 183 282 189 412 312  83 134 182  94 431 125 166  97  LEICESTER
372 208 269  88  78 207 170  88 192 178  76  52  41 206 247 241 376 276 135 152 196  44 402 132 140  70  52  LINCOLN
333 102 206  99  67 267 170 179 169 115 113  87  89 294 206 240 313 213 142 243  95 126 361 236  75  73 110 118  LIVERPOOL
335 128 208  87  37 252 167 159 188 117  99  59  50 273 209 315 215 122 123 121  98 363 211  72  43  95  85  33  MANCHESTER
271 232 185 174  68 316 265 196 287  94 175 130  82 316 146 337 278 192 230 262 224  87 300 253  80  62 154 125 134 104  MIDDLESBROUGH
232 261 149 209  98 345 300 232 312  58 209 165 115 350 106 360 239 237 139 263 296 257 123 259 287  89  96 188 153 167 136  38  NEWCASTLE
476 270 371 163 185 174 229  62 256 280 142 136 142 106  35 268 145 505  43 249 178 112 101 210 177 221 252  NORWICH
381 155 279  53  78 191 140  84 165 188  50  15  46 210 256 232 386 286 106 148 177  83 410 140 141  72  28  37 103  67 128 159 118  NOTTINGHAM
485 151 358  61 167 106  72  92 106 267  56  99 138 143 358 151 465 365  50 134 207 169 513 128 223 162  75 123 168 157 218 253 159 102  OXFORD
680 310 553 273 394 279 181 343 230 463 278 325 369 355 551 111 602 355 201 338 415 401 715 375 419 391 301 353 342 351 449 481 396 324 261  PENZANCE
 84 362  92 336 245 486 412 370 415 137 346 309 254 485  43 487 104  58 377 439 362 271 112 424 181 233 326 290 252 254 189 148 394 298 404 598  PERTH
616 241 485 203 325 206 113 274 159 394 209 254 300 284 485  43 592 490 150 305 322 332 648 305 348 323 231 283 282 281 379 412 328 255 193  74 529  PLYMOUTH
575 217 448 147 254  47  92 132 138 357 132 175 231 123 448 117 581 291 253 603 158 308 247 166 209 293 273 572 162 276 230 136 189 235 201 288 320 190 162  65 217 461 146  20  46  23 206 177  SOUTHAMPTON
520 258 431 152 220  85 177  63 211 340 129 156 206  85 395 226 548 438 151  61 313 200 549  57 283 213 139 156 256 225 278 299  99 160 106 337 439 265 111 106 145 207 200 194 127  SOUTHEND
368 112 241  44  73 217 127 137 140 150  62  32  74 236 241 202 348 248  94 123 117 396 179 121  79  55  87  56  38 141 176 171  50 105 313 287 241 201 147 159  51  35 183 192  STOKE
504  74 377 124 220 218  81 236  41 286 139 163 229 264 377 154 484 384  91 279 202 260 532 279 241 225 163 217 166 187 289 320 286 178 144 266 423 196 174 147 136 203 124 155 277 159  SWANSEA
212 588 310 557 461 728 644 589 659 354 563 529 477 703 170 726 604 657 589 492 108 406 998 453 539 510 469 471 408 368 613 518 621 823 221 756 711 662 663 492 526 680 657 504 640  THURSO
431  95 304  30 135 162  63 119  73 213  43  68 117 197 304 136 411 311  29 181 151 166 459 174 169 146 118 113 103 197 229 180  84  57 248 350 177 166  95 105 105  48 124 158  69  97 567  WORCESTER
312 211 207 129  34 269 227 151 237 116 129  84  33 269 187 289 314 214 181 213 184  37 342 214  85  24 108  73  96  66  48  83 176  84 174 400 230 331 267 223 244  53 136 244 214 114 256 449 164  YORK
497 205 396 118 202  53 117  57 151 305 107 126 163  73 372 170 503 403 102  79 260 185 527  76 264 195 101 132 205 185 245 276 114 126  54 282 416 214  74  39  97 165 160  76  43 165 188 634 106 207  LONDON
```

LIMITED INTERCHANGE MOTORWAY JUNCTIONS

M1

Junction 2
Northbound: No exit, access from A1 only
Southbound: No access, exit to A1 only

Junction 4
Northbound: No exit, access from A41 only
Southbound: No access, exit to A41 only

Junction 6a
Northbound: No exit, access from M25 only
Southbound: No access, exit to M25 only

Junction 7
Northbound: No exit, access from M10 only
Southbound: No access, exit to M10 only

Junction 17
Northbound: No access, exit to M45 only
Southbound: No exit, access from M45 only

Junction 19
Northbound: Exit to M6 only
Southbound: Access from M6 only

Junction 35a
Northbound: No access, exit to A616 only
Southbound: No exit, access from A616 only

Junction 44
Northbound: No exit, access only
Southbound: No access, exit only

Junction 45
Northbound: No access, exit to A61 only
Southbound: No exit, access from A61 only

Junction 46
Southbound: No access from A61

Junction 47
Northbound: No access from A653, exit only
Southbound: No access or exit

End of Motorway.
Northbound: Exit to M621 south-westbound
  only (M621 junction 3)

M2

Junction 1
Eastbound: Access from A2 eastbound only
Westbound: Exit to A2 westbound only

M3

Junction 8
Westbound: No access, exit to A303 only
Eastbound: No exit, access from A303 only

Junction 13
Southbound: No access from A335 onto
M3 leading to M27 eastbound

M4

Junction 1
Westbound: Access from A4 westbound only
Eastbound: Exit to A4 eastbound only

Junction 29
Westbound: No access, exit to A48(M) only
Eastbound: No exit, access from A48(M) only

Junction 38
Westbound: No access, exit to A48 only

Junction 39
Westbound: No exit, access from A48 only
Eastbound: No exit or access

Junction 41
Westbound: No exit, access from A48 only
Eastbound: No access, exit to A48 only

Junction 46
Westbound: No access, exit to A48 only
Eastbound: No exit, access from A48 only

M5

Junction 10
Southbound: No access, exit to A4019 only
Northbound: No exit, access from A4019 only

Junction 12
Southbound: No exit, access from A38 only
Northbound: No access, exit to A38 only

Junction 29
Southbound: No exit, access from A30 only
Northbound: No access, exit to A30 only

M6

Junction 4
Northbound: No exit to M42 northbound
            No access from M42 southbound
Southbound: No exit to M42
            No access from M42 southbound

Junction 4a
Northbound: No exit, access from M42
  southbound only
Southbound: No access, exit to M42 only

Junction 5
Northbound: No access, exit to A452 only
Southbound: No exit, access from A452 only

Junction 10a
Northbound: No access, exit to M54 only
Southbound: No exit, access from M54 only

Junction 20
Northbound: No exit to M56 eastbound
Southbound: No access from M56 westbound

Junction 24
Northbound: No exit, access from A58 only
Southbound: No access, exit to A58 only

Junction 25
Northbound: No access, exit to A49 only
Southbound: No exit, access from A49 only

Junction 30
Northbound: No exit, access from M61
  northbound only
Southbound: No access, exit to M61
  southbound only

M8

Junction 3
Westbound and eastbound:
  Exit to A899 southbound only
  Access from A899 northbound only

Junction 8
Westbound: No access from M73 southbound
Eastbound: No exit to M73 northbound

Junction 9
Westbound: No exit, access only
Eastbound: No access, exit only

Junction 14
Westbound: No exit, access only
Eastbound: No access, exit only

Junction 16
Westbound: No access, exit only
Eastbound: No exit, access only

Junction 17
Westbound: No access, exit to A82 only
Eastbound: No exit, access from A82 only

Junction 18
Westbound: No access, exit only

Junction 19
Westbound: No access from A814 westbound
Eastbound: No exit to A814 eastbound

Junction 20
Westbound: No access, exit only
Eastbound: No exit, access only

Junction 21
Westbound: No exit, access only
Eastbound: No access, exit only

Junction 22
Westbound: No access, exit to M77 only
Eastbound: No exit, access from M77 only
Junction 23
Westbound: No access, exit to B768 only
Eastbound: No exit, access from B768 only
Junction 25
Westbound and eastbound:
 Exit to A739 northbound only
 Access from A739 southbound only

M9

Junction 1
Northbound: No access, exit to A8000 only
Southbound: No exit, access from A8000 only
Junction 2
Northbound: No exit, access from B8046 only
Southbound: No access, exit to B8046 only
Junction 3
Northbound: No access, exit to A803 only
Southbound: No exit, access from A803 only
Junction 6
Northbound: No exit, access only
Southbound: No access, exit to A905 only
Junction 8
Northbound: No access, exit to M876 only
Southbound: No exit, access from M876 only

M10

Junction with M1 (M1 Junction 7)
Northbound: No exit to M1 southbound
Southbound: No access from M1 northbound

M11

Junction 4
Northbound: No exit, access from A406
 eastbound only
Southbound: No access, exit to A406
 westbound only
Junction 5
Northbound: No access, exit to A1168 only
Southbound: No exit, access from A1168 only
Junction 9
Northbound: No access, exit only
Southbound: No exit, access only
Junction 13
Northbound: No access, exit only
Southbound: No exit, access only

Junction 14
Northbound: No access from A45 eastbound
 No exit to A45 westbound
Southbound: No exit, access from A45
 eastbound only

M20

Junction 2
Eastbound: No access, exit to A20 only
 (access via M26 Junction 2a)
Westbound: No exit, access only
 (exit via M26 Junction 2a)
Junction 3
Eastbound: No exit, access from M26
 eastbound only
Westbound: No access, exit to M26
 westbound only
Junction 11a
Westbound: No exit to Eurotunnel
Eastbound: No access from Eurotunnel

M23

Junction 7
Southbound: No access from A23 northbound
Northbound: No exit to A23 southbound

M25

Junction 5
Clockwise: No exit to M26 eastbound
Anti-clockwise: No access from M26
 westbound
Spur to A21
Southbound: No access from M26 westbound
Northbound: No exit to M26 eastbound
Junction 19
Clockwise: No access exit only
Anti-clockwise: No exit access only
Junction 21
Clockwise and Anti-clockwise:
 No exit to M1 southbound
 No access from M1 northbound
Junction 31
Southbound: No exit access only
 (exit via Junction 30)
Northbound: No access exit only
 (access via Junction 30)

M26

Junction with M25
Westbound: No exit to M25 anti-clockwise
 or spur to A21 southbound
Eastbound: No access from M25 clockwise
 or spur to A21 northbound

Junction with M20 (M20 Junction 3)
Eastbound: No exit to M20 westbound
Westbound: No access from M20 eastbound

M27

Junction 4
Eastbound and westbound: No exit to A33
 southbound (Southampton)
 No access from A33 northbound
Junction 10
Eastbound: No exit, access from A32 only
Westbound: No access, exit to A32 only

M40

Junction 3
North-westbound: No access,
 exit to A40 only
South-westbound: No exit,
 access from A40 only
Junction 7
South-eastbound: No exit, access only
North-westbound: No access, exit only
Junction 13
South-eastbound: No exit, access only
North-westbound: No access, exit only
Junction 14
South-eastbound: No access, exit only
North-westbound: No exit, access only
Junction 16
South-eastbound: No access, exit only
North-westbound: No exit, access only

M42

Junction 1
Eastbound: No exit
Westbound: No access
Junction 7
Northbound: No access, exit to M6 only
Southbound: No exit, access from M6
 northbound only
Junction 8
Northbound: No exit, access from M6
 southbound only
Southbound: Exit to M6 northbound only
 Access from M6 southbound only

M45

Junction with M1
Eastbound: No exit to M1 northbound
Westbound: No access from M1 southbound

Junction with A45 east of dunchurch
Eastbound: No access, exit only
Westbound: No exit, access from northbound
 of A45 only

86

M53

Junction 11

Southbound and northbound: No access from M56 eastbound, no exit to M56 westbound

M56

Junction 1

Westbound: No access from M63 south-eastbound
No access from A34 northbound
Eastbound: No exit to M63 north-westbound
No exit to A34 southbound

Junction 2

Westbound: No access, exit to A560 only
Eastbound: No exit, access from A560 only

Junction 3

Westbound: No exit, access only
Eastbound: No access, exit only

Junction 4

Westbound: No access, exit only
Eastbound: No exit, access only

Junction 7

Westbound: No access, exit only

Junction 8

Westbound: No exit, access from A556 only
Eastbound: No access, no exit

Junction 9

Westbound: No exit to M6 southbound
Eastbound: No access from M6 northbound

Junction 15

Westbound: No access from M53
Eastbound: No exit to M53

M57

Junction 3

Northbound: No exit, access only
Southbound: No access, exit only

Junction 5

Northbound: No exit, access from A580 westbound only
Southbound: No access, exit to A580 eastbound only

M58

Junction 1

Eastbound: No exit, access from A506 only
Westbound: No access, exit to A506 only

M61

Junctions 2 and 3

North-westbound:
No access from A580 eastbound
No access from Motorway spur (A666)
Sth.-eastbound: No exit to A580 westbound

Junction 9

North-westbound:
No access, exit only
South-eastbound:
No exit, access only

Junction with M6 (M6 Junction 30)

North-westbound:
No exit to M6 southbound
South-eastbound:
No access from M6 northbound

M62

Junction 14

Eastbound: No exit to A580
No access from A580 westbound
Westbound: No exit to A580 eastbound
No access from A580

Junction 15

Eastbound: No exit, access from A666 only
Westbound: No access, exit to A666 only

Junction 23

Eastbound: No access, exit to A640 only
Westbound: No exit, access from A640 only

M63

Junction 9

South-eastbound: No access from or exit to A5103 northbound
North-westbound: No access from or exit to A5103 southbound

Junction 10

South-eastbound: No exit to A34 northbound or to M56. No access from A34 southbound
North-westbound: No exit to A34 northbound
No access from A34 southbound or M56

Junction 11

Nth.-eastbound: No access, exit to A560 only
Sth.-westbound: No exit, access from A560 only

Junction 13

North-eastbound: No access, exit only
South-westbound: No exit, access only

Junction 14

North-eastbound: No access or exit

Junction 15

South-westbound: No access from A560/A6017

M65

Junction 9

Nth.-eastbound: No access, exit to A679 only
Sth.-westbound: No exit, access from A679 only

Junction 11

North-eastbound: No exit, access only
South-westbound: No access, exit only

M66

Junction 1

Southbound: No exit, access from A56 only
Northbound: No access, exit to A56 only

Junction 12

Northbound: No exit
Southbound: No access

M67

Junction 1

Eastbound: No access, exit to A6017 only
Westbound: No exit, access from A6017 only

Junction 2

Eastbound: No exit, access from A57 only
Westbound: No access, exit to A57 only

M69

Junction 2

North-eastbound:
No exit, access from A5070 only
South-westbound: No access, exit to A5070 only

M73

Junction 1

Northbound: No access from A721 westbound
Southbound: No exit to A721 eastbound

Junction 2

Northbound: No access from M8 eastbound
No exit to A89 eastbound
Southbound: No exit to M8 westbound
No access from A89 westbound

Junction 3

Northbound: No exit to A80 south-westbound
Southbound:
No access from A80 north-eastbound

M74

Junction 7

Southbound: No access, exit to A72 only
Northbound: No exit, access from A72 only

Junction 9

Southbound: No access, exit to A74 only
Northbound: No access, no exit

Junction 10

Southbound: No exit, access from A74 only

Junction 11

Southbound: No access, exit to A74 only
Northbound: No exit, access from A74 only

Junction 12

Southbound: Exit to A74 southbound only
Northbound: Access from A74 northbound only

M77

Junction with M8 (M8 Junc. 22)
Northbound: No exit to M8 westbound
Southbound: No access from M8 eastbound

M80

Junction 5
Northbound: No access from M876
Southbound: No exit to M876

M90

Junction 7
Northbound: No exit, access from A91 only
Southbound: No access, exit to A91 only
Junction 8
Northbound: No access, exit to A91 only
Southbound: No exit, access from A91 only
Junction 10
Northbound: No access from A912
        Exit to A912 northbound only
Southbound: No exit to A912
        Access from A912 southbound only

M180

Junction 1
Eastbound: No access, exit only
Westbound: No exit, access from A18 only

M606

Junction with Merrydale Road, Bradford
Northbound: No access, exit only

M876

Junction with M80
        (M80 Junction 5)
North-eastbound:
        No access from M80 southbound
South-westbound: No exit to M80 northbound
Junction 2
North-eastbound: No access, exit only
South-westbound: No exit, access only
Junction with M9 (M9 Junc. 8)
North-eastbound: No exit to M9 northbound
South-westbound:
        No access from M9 southbound

A1(M) (Hertfordshire Section)

Junction 2
Southbound: No exit, access from A1001 only
Northbound: No access, exit only
Junction 3
Southbound: No access, exit only
Junction 5
Northbound: No exit, access only
Southbound: No exit or access

A1(M) (Durham Section)

Junction with A66(M) SW of Darlington
Northbound: No access, exit to A66(M) only
Southbound: No exit, access from A66(M)
Junction with A1 Gateshead Western By-Pass
Northbound: Exit to A1 North-westbound, and to A194(M)
Southbound: Access from A1 South-eastbound, and from A194(M)

A3(M)

Junction with Purbrook Wy., Havant
Northbound: No access, exit only
Southbound: No exit, access only

A38(M) Aston Expressway

Junction with Victoria Road, Aston
Northbound: No access, exit only
Southbound: No exit, access only

A40(M) Westway

Junction at Royal Oak
Eastbound: No access, exit to Westbourne Terrace and A404 Harrow Road
Westbound: No exit, access from Gloucester Terrace only
Junction at Western end of Marylebone Flyover
Eastbound: No exit, access from A404 Harrow Road eastbound only
Westbound: No access, exit to A404 Harrow Road westbound only

A48(M)

Junction with M4 (M4 Junction 29)
South-westbound: access from M4 westbound
North-eastbound: exit to M4 eastbound only
Junction 29a
South-westbound: Exit to A48 westbound only
North-eastbound:
        Access from A48 eastbound only

A57(M) Mancunian Way

Junction with A34 Brook Street, Manchester
Eastbound: No access, exit to A34 Brook Street southbound only
Westbound: No exit, access only

A58(M) Leeds Inner Ring Road

Junction with Park Lane/Westgate
Southbound: No access, exit only

A64(M) Leeds Inner Ring Road (Continuation of A58(M))

Junction with A58 Clay Pit Lane
Eastbound: No Access
Westbound: No exit

A66(M)

Junction with A1(M) SW of Darlington
South-westbound:
        Exit to A1(M) southbound only
North-eastbound:
        Access from A1(M) northbound only

A102(M) Blackwall Tunnel Southern Approach

Junction with A2203 Blackwall Lane
Northbound: No exit, access from A2203 Blackwall Lane only

A167(M) Newcastle Central Motorway

Junction with Camden Street
Northbound: No exit, access only
Southbound: No exit or access

A194(M)

Junction with A1(M) and A1 Gateshead Western By-Pass
Southbound: Exit to A1(M) only
Northbound: Access from A1(M) only